In the Company of Light

The Concord Library
John Elder, Series Editor

IN THE

COMPANY

OF LIGHT

JOHN HAY

Beacon Press   Boston

Beacon Press
25 Beacon Street
Boston, Massachusetts 02108-2892
http://www.beacon.org

Beacon Press books
are published under the auspices of
the Unitarian Universalist Association of Congregations.

02 01 00 99 98   8 7 6 5 4 3 2

Text design by Sara Eisenman
Composition by Wilsted & Taylor Publishing Services

Library of Congress Cataloging-in-Publication Data

Hay, John, 1915–
    In the company of light / John Hay.
        p. cm. — (A Concord Library)
    ISBN 0-8070-8538-3 (cloth)
    ISBN 0-8070-8539-1 (paper)
    1. Nature.   2. Natural history—Maine.   I. Title.
    II. Series.
    QH81.H368   1998   97-14415
    508.741—dc21

To John (Jack) Putnam Hay and a future filled with wings

Contents

1

The Turning Year   3

Fox and Goldenrod   24

Watchers   36

Windows on Space   48

Tern Islands   55

2

A Loss of Neighbors   71

Power and Light   84

A Shining Fish   99

Metamorphic Time   105

The Source of the Brook   120

The Sea in the Land   137

The Way to the Salt Marsh   149

Life in Space   159

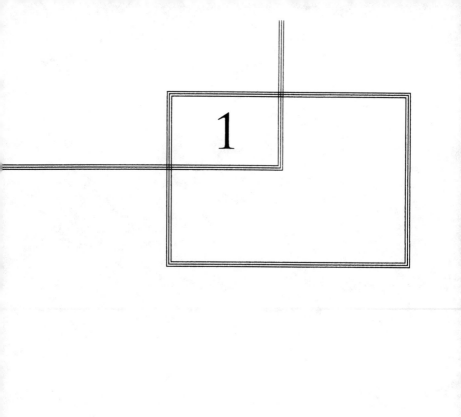

1

The Turning Year

A nother summer is moving out along the coast of Maine, with its innumerable islands, its swirling currents and flowing tides. Once again, I hang on the balance of our star now turning against the sun. I am able to see, from the vantage point of our old house and barn, a world of travelers responding to new imperatives of the changing season. It is early in September, and the barn swallows, nesting in the barn rafters overhead where I am writing, are almost entirely gone. I have let them in for many years, opening the back window of the loft, and I have always rejoiced in their company, which is as real to me as any other I have experienced in my life. Their timing is perfect. Their attention to their responsibilities is unswerving, and their skill in hunting for food over the nearby waters is exact, dynamic, and superbly adapted to a mercurial atmosphere. I am always reassured, when I listen to their warbly, intermittent chattering, that they are more intensely involved than I had ever hoped to be. I can't put these birds apart from me because I have inherited some elevated position from which I can look down on them, with impunity. I am only half engaged, at best, with their complex alliances with this hemisphere, the sun and moon, and all the subtle currents of their surroundings. I can only wonder at how far removed, almost inoperable, our own senses have become by comparison.

The swallows begin to disappear again, with an inner timing that follows a timeless sea. They join thousands of others, flitting fast through the fiery lungs of the air, at times landing, relocating and feeding, dipping and rising. Come back again Sister Swallow, as the poet Shelley called them. Come back to relocate us in the sea reaches of our home.

The great fetch of the tides has its limits on these shores, where they move in and back out of Broad Cove beyond us, a half an hour or more by boat from the open sea. Below the high bank on which our house is located is a tidal inlet where a sawmill was built in the eighteenth century. Nothing is left of it now but piles of rock on the opposing banks. Past Broad Cove, the tides end in two wide, tributary streams that lose themselves in salt marsh grasses, sloping fields, and wooded banks.

In the cove at low tide, great blue herons stab

at crabs and small fish, and the tide pools stream with eel grass. The rocks are encrusted with barnacles, and in between them are banks of blue mussels which reached maturity before being suffocated by the weight of numbers. The sea is always streaming in on the tides to suggest the vast dimensions of its powers to replenish or remove. The rocky shores and their spiraling spruce trees are rooted in its restraint and its everlasting storms.

At extreme low tide, when muddy flats are uncovered, the local people for over three centuries have been digging for soft-shell clams. Clams were one of those resources, like so many others, that was said to be inexhaustible, but the demand for them has never slowed down and both clams and clammers are becoming scarce. It is a testimony to the prolific nature of the clam that any should be left at all.

The lobster boats are plying the waters, their droning engines slowing down, then starting up again, as the traps are pulled up. The lobstermen seem to be thriving and having no trouble meeting the immense demand for lobsters in restaurants up and down the coast. Why have lobsters held up so well? It has been suggested that the great fish such as salmon and cod which once fed on young lobsters are now fished out. The ground fishes off the coast have almost dropped

out of sight in recent years. Relentless technolog-
ical improvements to the fishing fleets of New
England and Canada made it impossible for any
fish to hide from view, and without adequate
limits on how much they could catch, fishermen
soon ran out of fish to chase. Once thriving fishing establishments along the coast have failed,
one after another. With breathtaking speed, an
insatiable economy now threatens to move in
and neutralize what is left of the local identity, as
developers scoop up the empty waterfronts with
plans to improve them into shops and restaurants. The local fishing and farming communities are more and more dispossessed, though the
farms are not yet entirely gone and many families
bear names that go back to when their forefathers
dug in centuries ago. Yet this magnificent coastline born of the North Atlantic is of a stature that
will outlast us.

A quiet summer was welcome, away from the
loud and lethal velocity of the turnpike sending its hundreds of thousands on temporary vis-
its to the north. We busied ourselves with occasional fishing expeditions after mackerel on
Broad Cove. We encouraged swallows, watched
butterflies and fireflies, and raised vegetables using shoreline wrack for mulch and fertilizer. It
amounts to a renewal of the unfinished dialogue
with sea and shore that so many settlers left be-

hind them. Americans became a nation of itinerants, always moving away from the place they started with, and trying to compensate for it with substitutes that seldom took root. There is a chance here, at least, to hang upon the north stars, and steer our way along the infinite avenues of the Milky Way.

A few weeks ago, I met a man named Matthew Smith at a crafts fair on the lower slopes of Mt. Sunapee in New Hampshire. He was selling prints and paintings of fish at one of the booths that the big tents enclosed. He told me that he had captained his own vessel, an eighty-foot trawler, at the age of twenty-one, working over the famous fishing grounds of Georges Bank, one of the richest such areas in the world. This was during the early '70s, and during the years that followed, he watched the waters growing browner and cloudier. They were also increasingly littered with waste from the land: trash, plastic, garbage, oil slicks—the waste and trash from the growing cities and their industries. Also in the '70s, a vast tonnage of fish was being lifted and scoured from the ocean floor by factory vessels from many nations that processed everything they caught on board. The ground fish—cod, haddock, halibut, yellowtail flounder—began to disappear. By the mid to late '80s, there were no longer enough fish to sustain a livelihood, and Matt left for the hills. The bottom had dropped out, and in a surprisingly short period of time. A stressed marine ecosystem was simply being starved to death, on a scale that seemed incomprehensible to those who had inherited the deep-seated idea that the ocean was inexhaustible. And so, Matt Smith quit fishing to draw pictures of fish in the hills of New Hampshire. He spoke of greed and population growth as factors contributing to the loss of the fish; it might also come down to a matter of inattention on a major scale. A society driven primarily by economic motives, seeing resources as values to be measured in terms of profit and loss, does not know one species from another. Essential distinctions in life are lost sight of in the pursuit of abstractions. You ought to know your own prey in order to save its life, as well as your own.

"Everything has a right to be left alone," he said, "even rocks and trees."

I left him with his regenerating art, after buying a print of a black, or big-mouth, bass from him, the kind I used to go after with hook, line, and sinker on Lake Sunapee many years ago. They remain a shining measure of my existence.

In that small and cramped booth at the crafts fair, Matt Smith also displayed a small print, in color, of the Perseid meteor showers. Having seen loads of flashing, slippery bodies of herring being pulled out of inland waters, I wondered if there had not been times, under magnificent clear nights over the ocean, when he compared that great abundance of the waters beneath his boat with star showers raining from the heavens.

Georges Bank has now been partly closed to fishing, in the hope, if not the expectation, that a fair percentage of its former abundance might return. Modern society has been blinded in its assumption that advanced methods and technologies, backed by money, might be able, not only to exploit a resource to its limits, but to restore what it destroys. There is no collaboration between humans and fishes when thousands of fishing communities from here to Labrador are forced into bankruptcy, and torn from their moral, physical, and spiritual dependence on a primal source of food. Local cultures, whose customs and speech were born of an intimacy with the sea, are replaced by words without attachment. How could these great shores, on both sides of the Atlantic, with their ancient and powerful hold on humanity, have been so carelessly and ignorantly cut off from our connections with them?

Our replacements, in word or speech, are hardly worth the paper they are written on. Even here, on this back shore, lying steadfast in the tides, there is a palpable sense of emptiness. Many of those now moving into the region have no skills but those they borrow through mechanical aids, and their hands seem to have no hold on the roots that surround them. The primal sources of life will only return as we learn how to accommodate them.

It is one thing to be "lost at sea," in the ancient if tragic sense of the term. It is another matter to be out of contact with it, as the following eloquently suggests:

> I've tried at different meetings to express what it's like, but I guess the best way to describe what it's like is the fact that in Newfoundland today, even after a year, many people cannot talk about it. They find it hard to articulate their feelings. People who have spent their whole life talking about nothing else but fish don't want to talk about it. They'll talk about hockey scores, crises in Bosnia—about anything but the loss they are going through.
>
> So what is the loss? First, it is the recognition that given the power structure, we fishermen were —and are—helpless. As a group, we are political eunuchs. We have no power.
>
> More fundamentally, we know that we have allowed great damage to be done to the one thing that kept our society together—the ecosystem that

we were living off. If you ask older fishermen in Newfoundland, they will tell you that they don't expect to see a commercial fishery in Newfoundland ever again, that it is gone forever. There are others—and I am included among them—who take a more optimistic view of the tremendous healing powers of the ocean. But whether we will be given a second chance is a question over which we have no control. It's a process that must surely teach us something; if not, then we are incapable of learning.[1]

Recently, I saw hanging in a local gallery a print made by a Canadian artist. In it men and women were seated around a communal table, following an old custom in Nova Scotia of coming together for a feast in celebration of the annual fish harvest. What was most apparent in this picture was a silence. All the guests wore somber expressions and dark clothes. Just as eloquent were the plates in front of them. They were completely empty. Judas Iscariot was nowhere to be seen. Perhaps we can all bear that name.

Day by day, we idly watch the calendar, while little happens there except passing appointments. The realities of the season are carried by light and

1. Cabot Martin, "A Black Hole in the Map of Hope," *The Island Journal* (the annual publication of the Island Institute), vol. 11.

air, streaming overhead like fingerling fishes along the summer shore. I carry our small one-man canoe down to the water to paddle to a point of land that marks a branch of tidewater reaching its limits in grasses and upland slopes. The banks are lined with spruce and pine and a few large red oaks. A bald eagle soars high overhead, while a big, solitary cloud moves slowly by, headed in a southerly direction.

This wide branch or inlet moves past fields and woodlands and finally ends in a narrow cut past rocky ledges on both banks, where the water at high tide, warmed by the sun, makes a perfect swimming hole. Alone this day, though I have been here with the family many times, I sit on the rock, watching the tide starting to run out, and listening to a light wind making music with the long-needled branches of the white pines. The smell of the fallen needles lying on the ground beside me carries the sweetness of all the New England summers of my life. This place has been a charmed circle for me, beyond which I have heard the beautiful, uplifted tones of the white-throated sparrow and the thrush. I could stay here until the fall of night, but I would lose the tide. So I jump in for a last swim, and a long float down the outgoing channel, and then head back to where I started from.

Another big cloud has come into being, out of

the multiple realignments in the atmosphere, floating overhead to be dissipated and absorbed in ocean weather. A few raindrops fall on the surface of the water, each creating its own circle. I am commanded by moving waters, subordinated to the will of a perpetually changing sky. I will return in order to go in, without self will. It is the indisputable mastery of such surroundings that measures us, and brings us its peace. Do not call it wilderness unless you are prepared to be lost and discovered there.

As late summer days start to merge with new cycles of heat and cold, I am reminded of my inability to catch up. This is a season for travel, and most of its participants, or local interpreters of change, have passed by me unseen, and out of reach. The harbor seals, not popular with local fishermen because they compete with them for fish, spend much of the summer on a rocky islet on the far side of Broad Cove. They, and all the other small populations throughout the islands, leave here for deeper waters along the coast by late August. The others fish in a channel that runs down the center of the relatively shallow cove, and haul out on the rocks, often at mid to high tide.

The seals inhabit a world I can read about but know very little. I have never been equipped for it. What fishing I do is from the surface. R. M.

Lockley wrote a book about British seals called *Grey Seal, Common Seal.* In it he discusses a seal's vision, which is, at the very least, startling to one whose vision is poor. Their large, round eyes suggest their ability, especially in pinpointing their prey in lighted waters. Yet blind seals are perfectly capable of fishing and finding their way.

The Weddell seal of the Antarctic can dive down to a depth of fifteen hundred feet in complete darkness under the ice, where pressures are enormous, but it can "see." Seals are equipped with brushlike whiskers that can detect vibrations in the water, and have subcutaneous senses along their tubular bodies to help guide them. They are marvels, masters of a deeper part of the universe which is quite beyond my understanding. I am always held back by an inability to follow what I see; but see we must or gradually starve what senses we need to know the worlds we dimly occupy.

Different races of shorebirds, after nesting far to the north of us, have already put in an appearance and then flown away. Every year, I watch for a flock of black-bellied plovers to show up at much the same time and place on another far side of the cove. With a plover's way of moving forward, stopping, and then moving again, they are always ready and alert. Disturbed, they all speed off at once, with a sweet and plaintive cry. It is one of the more beautiful calls of fading summer. Sanderlings appear, with twinkling legs, to explore the mat of seaweed covering offshore rocks, or hurry over the edge of the mudflats at low tide. The bobbing and turning yellowlegs, wonderfully slender on their long legs, fly away, with their high whistling: "Follow. Follow." And follow is what I would love to do, though always stopped short by myself. They are all, each in its essential style, inner chronometers of an outer weather that governs vast reaches of territory, at all points of the compass, from here to the Arctic and down to the Southern Hemisphere.

The barn swallows, my overhead companions throughout the summer, may winter in Costa Rica or as far south as Argentina, flocking together and feeding along the way. The sanderlings may reach Tierra del Fuego. Their major flyways have been mapped by scientific teams and individual observers, and there have been many possible explanations of how birds can find their way. How the inner, navigational sense of a seabird or a sea turtle really works may eventually find a solution, but we are still on the outside looking in. Modern society is used to expecting rational answers to imponderable questions. I do not make up for it, as an amateur, by tolerating the swallows for a season. We are still at more

than arm's length from each other at the close of
it. But whatever there is in me that wants to follow other destinies, other pathways in living
things that reach beyond my own limitations,
must be satisfied for a while, in this company. If
you are in need of extensions, look no further
than what you find at home.

The swallow is a small bird with a great
coastal geography in its mind, as well as the signals of a sure return. Considered in this light, it is
surely not just a simple animal without reason-
ing power. It may know more than we do, who
have left so much inner attention to the earth behind us. It seems worth repeating that we learn
the most from what we are not.

The swallow nesting season is short. The
young grow with amazing rapidity, while the
adults are tireless in bringing them food, constantly flying out after insects which are often
scarce because of weather conditions. The intensity and single-minded devotion of these birds is
inspiring. They are as quick in their responses as
the light now shimmering over the water. They
hunt for insect food I am unable to see.

One day, a friend came by and watched the
birds for a while as they raced through the air,
swinging, turning tight corners, rising and falling after their prey. One of them came within
inches of the side of the barn, flying so fast that he

thought it might crash. The thought occurred to me later that this could describe a major difference between swallows and the human race. They knew how not to hit the barn.

Some of the swallows, having been successfully reared to the point that they can fly away and feed for themselves, may have left the barn weeks ago. A few are still being fed at the nest. Many of the fledged birds do not head south right away but range over coastal waterways not too many miles distant. One day, when there were only a very few still left in the barn, a flock of up to fifty flew in from over the islands to land on the barn roof. At the clap of my hands, they all flew up and fanned out to disappear in the distance.

Out of nineteen nests, our summer count, with three or four chicks in each one, plus a number of second broods, and discounting some casualties among them, a hundred swallows might have grown up and flown out. So if this flock of fifty were not just visitors, a passing flock from another locality, their purpose might be one of recognition. Swallows do return periodically, at the end of a season, to where they were originally born and teased into feeding by their parents. So a fidelity to the nesting site is reinforced and stays in their memory until they return again. So, in a way, they strengthen a fidelity in me.

A timing which does not follow either the

news of the day or the clock moves out, or reappears, in response to transformations we are unable to pin down. The brassy call of a blue jay in the trees reminds me of colder days to come. Every year a kingfisher, or a pair of them, has come in toward the end of August, staying for a week or so to fish on the marsh minnows or other kinds that run in with the oncoming tide. One of them now perches on the mast of our small sailing boat. From there it makes slanting dives and returns with its food, and a rattling cry. This is not only a repeated event I may be able to count on every year, but a blue opening into space. Kingfisher-blue, varying according to the species, is known to people of many countries, an overworld translation of sight and freedom.

The surrounding world of waters is full of shades and disguises that do not simply protect their wearers but mark the entrances of a past no longer visible. The great blue heron, whose heavy nests adorn a few of the outer islands, comes in to feed periodically on the low or ebbing tide, using its long, formidable beak as if throwing a spear to catch crabs and fishes. With those glaring yellow, expressionless eyes and extended neck—a flying lizard out of the age of dinosaurs—it also acts for an aggressive past that means to stay, ignoring our dismissal of it.

One tall, patient heron stands like a statue

waiting for its chance, and a second one comes in, invading its territory. The first one then chases off the intruder, both of them raising their great wings, while squawking, harsh and loud. Two yellowlegs, which have been bobbing and teetering nearby, in nervous agitation, suddenly take alarm at this flurry between giants, and speed away.

Yesterday becomes tomorrow, and the next day comes too soon. I am dependent on a daily routine, with marked intervals, to mark the passage of time, but it escapes me into sunlight and shadow. We are far too slow to take in the measureless instruments of the sun. The birds, on the other hand, both in their quickness and obedience to its dictates, take time away with them, leaving me behind.

This is a season for travelers, after all, some of which are being hatched in the grass. Emergences and departures follow the annual process of change, in which there is untold mystery. That newly fledged birds of many species should take off and fly toward regions they have never seen, seems to require more reasons than a short season and a waning food supply. How many millions of years lie in these great migrations? How many drifting continents have contributed to their consistency?

Constant predation over the millennia may have contributed to quickness and spontaneity in birds. The impulse to escape is always genuine. But they do not safeguard their lives to the extent that they are not ready to lose them. Their impulses, not devoid of conscious determination, are never far removed from what the sentient earth requires of them. All life, physically and spiritually engaged with the earth's own migration, proceeds past the natural limits of its own conditions.

Some of the outer islands of Maine serve as resting as well as jumping-off places for birds on migration. Pete Noyes, of the Damariscotta River Association, took me out in his power boat—it is mid September—to two small islands south of Pemaquid Point, facing the open Atlantic. One is named Thrumcap, after an old nautical term, and the other is Outer White. We landed on Outer White, where a few spruce trees dwarfed by punishing winds and salt spray grow in the shelter of rock crevices and small ravines. Hardy plants are there, such as yarrow, nightshade, goldenrod, and aster. Rocky slopes led up to a central knoll, or island crest, marked by a single chimney. A man on the shore, at Christmas Cove, had told us that there was a small cottage there, which had recently been burned to the ground. He had seen it suddenly exploding on

the horizon, a fireball, like the rising sun. Although he was not caught, it was suspected that
the arsonist was a man with a local reputation for
mild lunacy. While the lone chimney marked the
passage of a sailing vessel out on the ocean, we
watched the birds around us as they flitted here
and there in the shelter of rocks and thickets.

Bay-breasted warblers were there as well as
yellowthroats, myrtles, and magnolias, and we
caught sight of a single cedar waxwing in the center of the island, perched on a branch. Two gray-
winged merlins cruised by one side of the island,
and a flicker screamed as it dropped down into
the safety of the undergrowth. Monarch butterflies, another famous far-ranging migrant, were
floating and alighting over parts of the island.
We now know that the monarchs winter in a
mountainous region of Mexico. The warblers
may have been heading for Central America, and
local songbirds might be erratic in their movements; but all were part of a greater company of
seasonal relocating, often over great distances
between a home nest and winter ranges. I suppose many of the long-distance migrants could
be called driven, from our perspective of self-
determination, aware of the risks ahead, but they
are profoundly engaged, on a continental scale,
and over the seas. Even on this small dot on the
map, with its tiny fraction of a much greater

company of travelers, I felt a commitment in them which raced ahead of my understanding.

Warblers on migration, while following the direct instinctive course of their inheritance, are beaten from it by storms and high winds. Some of those out to sea and following the coastline may be blown to land exhausted on the shore, where they can be easily picked up and swallowed by herring or black-back gulls. Others, on both sides of the Atlantic, have been forced down onto the decks of ships, where they lie, patches of sunlit color on their wings: yellow, orange, red, or green, a complex alliance with the spectrum of forest trees. Their inner lives turn as the earth turns, on a course with mystery.

In recent years, a number of these islands have been selected and acquired for conservation, and put out of reach of commercial exploitation. Some are managed for the study and protection of nesting birds, such as terns, cormorants, eiders, puffins, and guillemots. They are also essential in the lives of ospreys, great blue herons, and bald eagles, which feed in the tidal shores around them, the customary, if not unfailing riches of the shallow seas.

Perhaps these islands, with varying degrees of exposure to the storms and power of the North Atlantic, might serve another useful purpose. They could provide lessons in essentials for those who no longer know what it is to live with them. Whenever I have visited them over the years, I leave a man-contested world behind me, on automated travel, unlike the birds, using all its smoke and mirrors to disguise reality. We travel everywhere, landing nowhere. Out there, on the stripped-down outposts, there is primal honesty. Where the ever-watchful birds sit on their nests, feed their chicks, roost on the rocks, or forage over the waters after fish, there can be no separation from the genius of the ocean. Life thrives or starves in its presence. The birds feel its changing moods. They are constantly aware of its directions. A silvery gray and white tern holding a fish in its bill, presenting it in courtship to a mate, or feeding it to a chick at the nest, is the center of an indivisible world, and in that it speaks for all of us, on all our islands.

Fox and Goldenrod

The entirety of things calls out on the wind, as the seabirds are called by the voices of the sea. A few common and arctic terns, weeks after their nesting season is over, still fly in to hunt for small fish in the inlet below our house, and then are gone in early September. They have wonderfully lithe, vibrant bodies, capable of long periods of fishing without rest, and of flying for thousands of miles over coastal waters and the open ocean. I, who am so slow to move, have always marveled at the quickness and energy of so small a bird. They slide in low and fast over the surface, looking like so many white, skipped stones. Their range and their intent seem far wider than my own. They fly ahead of my mind's ability to grasp them.

I followed them over the years at their nesting sites on both sides of the Atlantic, learning a little more each time I went, but they were always ahead of me. I never saw anything but a fraction of what they were capable of. It is not because of their weakness but our own, as a less controlled race, that their numbers have dropped to a dangerous extent. We seem to crowd them out with our own clumsiness and inattention to lifesaving detail. When these few appear again, crying out excitedly on their hunting expeditions, they strike me like showers of snow, or the light on the bank of a cloud.

Periodically, in these northern latitudes, the night opens beyond the cloudy atmosphere to a clear vision of the universe. No part of the sky is without its mass of stars. We need no telescope to confirm what comes to our eyes in the magnificence of light, so infinitely distant, and so close at hand. A planet floats low over the swallow's barn, like fish in the dark sea, and in the presence of the stars we are dignified again, leaving our humiliations and exclusion behind us.

In the early morning, when the mists begin to evaporate in the sunlight, a small flock of migratory birds moves slowly away from the shore like a fleet of sailing vessels, heading out beyond the known horizon. They have a mission, granted them by the waters, the wind, and the stars. The only way we can begin to feel the extent of their engagement in ourselves is to set sail, and follow after.

Each day must move forward through universal light and darkness, and can never be held up by the erratic course of human enterprise. Although we may be born to tragic reversals and circumstances, the very worst thing that can happen to us is to fall out of the great company of life on the planet.

I have much to look for and comparatively little to find, but what I really wait on are the transformations in common phenomena. It is not a fixed ecology that heightens my awareness but one that is continually on the move, eluding categories, like the colors on a butterfly's wing. What purpose do these transformations serve? I doubt that there are facts enough to explain them.

By night, the ground still smells with the sweetness of flowers and newly mown hay. In the eastern sky, the moon glows with the color of dark oranges. The summer dances of the fireflies are gone from the fields, though I have seen a few glowworms, like signal markers on the ground beside the road. A shore wind dies down and the principal sound is that of the rushing tide.

There is a narrow valley or cut below our house which bisects the down-sloping fields on either side of it. There is enough water flowing through it during early spring to maintain a small brook pitching off into saltwater, but it has largely dried up by midsummer. Some wild iris and reeds grow in the marshy valley that feeds it, and there, unexpectedly, a wild, uncultivated garden has emerged this summer. Tall clumps of white asters fill it like a long cloud, together with blue asters on the fringes, and yellow-orange goldenrod, pluming in the sun.

It may be that this new growth has something to do with the fact that the ground was cut over a few years back, but the growth was unforeseen. Consequently, the wild garden is richer and more beautiful in our sight. The flowers of the asters are like small pinwheels, with yellow micro-suns at their centers. The great propriety and spacing of these flowering plants is visited by a white admiral butterfly, now landing, with a white sash around its black wings. I drift away too soon from this community.

Back in 1935, sixty years ago, Donald Culross Peattie, the botanist, published a book called *An Almanac for Moderns*. It was not so modern as to run ahead of its subject, a day-by-day reflection of nature in a land that could still be admired and interpreted for its own sake, as a result of several centuries of dependence on it. Americans have often drawn personal fire from their confrontation with nature. Accommodation is left behind. But Peattie knew that in plants lay the unity of the continent.

In his entry for September 5, it is written:

First in the summer woods they begin with the lady aster, a dainty lavender, its leaves heart shaped. Then on the marsh the rush asters bloom, and so, species by species, they fill up the forests and fields and swamps, New England aster and brown-eyed wood aster with petals like curling lashes. The asters number thirty kinds in the blue hills and green river valleys that I can see from the top of the ridge above my house. The country over, there are hundreds of species.

In England they call them Michaelmas daisies—but Europe has no asters at which an American would look twice. In this our western world the asters stand all through autumn, shoulder to shoulder in forest, on prairie, from the Atlantic to California, climbing up to the snows of Shasta, creeping out upon the salt marshes of Delaware. Here some call the white ones frostflower, for they come as the frost comes, as a breath upon the landscape, a silver rime of chill flowering in the old age of the year. In the southern mountains they are hailed as "farewell-summer." Farewell to August, to burning days. Farewell to corn weather. Farewell to swallows, and to red Antares angry as venom in the Scorpion.

The asters have reached such a degree of complexity that it is hard for the botanists to distinguish between them. I own a handbook to the

flowers which lists twenty-three species of goldenrod, but since they too hybridize in nature it is
equally difficult to identify distinct individuals
of goldenrod. They reach from Newfoundland
to Saskatchewan, and from the eastern states to
California, in wetland, dry land, open fields, and
mountainsides. Goldenrod, like the asters, are
pollinated by the butterflies and other insects,
not by the wind, which spreads the seeds of
America's wild grasses, the tough-fisted plants
that hold down the sod, safeguarding the integrity of the land for millions of years.

I have always welcomed the goldenrod, one
of the great continental symbols of America.
(The fact that we chose a hothouse rose for the
national flower only locks us further into a hothouse culture.) Goldenrods are of an honorable
company, in an eternal alliance with the sun.
Originally, it was only one flower, running to
meet me through the light, before I began to
differentiate between some of the species, rough
or fine, that grow in the open fields and climb the
local hills. Just the other day I leaned down in
passing to sniff the flower of a tall and slender
specimen growing at the bottom of the slope behind our house. It smelled as sweet as honey, and
when I looked it up, I found that it was *Solidago
fragrans*. This was a notable day, after a lifetime
of absence, to be drawn in like a bee, but for the

first time. It was as if my early training and education had stopped at the water's edge, and prevented me from making the right connections in this metamorphic world.

So I have my chance to begin again, feeling and seeing, knowing the goldenrods, flat-topped blossoms, pluming rods, large and coarse in their growth, hard to uproot, or fine and slender, all sunny flowers, bold in their right, carrying on, as all plants do, as ceaseless dialogue with the fluid nature of their surroundings.

The fields are alive with late emergings, like the little black crickets jumping and flicking ahead of me as I walk. They are a current food of the red fox, judging by the content of the thin, dark scat which marks its trails.

We have a fox on the roofline of our house, a copper weather vane which springs to life as the wind changes, dancing as lightly as a blade of grass. It is the spirit of a fox, responding to a real animal who lives nearby but is seldom seen. One morning the fox and I watched each other briefly when it came out into the open. Otherwise, our encounters are rare, though I have caught its scent on occasion, as our paths crossed. The male urine smells slightly like a skunk, which has given foxes a bad reputation in some quarters as "spoilers," but this scent is no more unpleasant than that of skunk cabbage, or of the beautiful red trillium, once called "stinking Benjamin" by native New Englanders, whose purpose is to attract carrion flies for pollination in season. This fox fragrance is worth a pause for its alliances, if nothing else. If I were to hold my nose at every crossing, how could I meet the real leaders of this world?

The fox marks its territory, which is ample and provides for its every need. It has its den hidden in the woods, a good supply of water, and a wide view from field to sea. It can find crickets, grasshoppers, and an occasional unwary bird to eat, as well as red squirrels. Above all, our foxes can find an apparently unfailing supply of meadow voles, which riddle the field with their holes. When a neighbor, Ricky Parlin, mowed the back field a few years ago, he disturbed so many voles with his heavy machine that they were forced out for hundreds of yards, and he saw a fox carrying away four of them at one time in his snappy jaws.

After the snow melted last year tunnels were exposed in many places, perhaps because the voles had eaten the grasses down to their roots. The roof had caved in, and they were open to the sky. Their branching runways converged into one, which led downhill, to end at the high bank above the shore. Was this a short-run migration, comparable to that of the more far-ranging lemmings, impelled by population pressure? The reproductive capacity of voles might tempt you to think so. They can have three to five young in one litter, and produce three to four litters a year. To top that, the young can begin breeding in three weeks. My friend Helen Hays, director of the Great Gull Island Program for nesting terns, introduced some fat, brown voles to the island with the idea of reducing the vegetation. The terns preferred bare ground for their nests, which are little more than scrapes, and since the island is very small, Helen had determined to make it easier for the birds to increase in numbers. Importing voles was not entirely successful because, reproductive rate aside, they preferred grass to weeds and shrubs.

Potentially, vole numbers are astronomical, meeting the extremes of the elements as well as the needs of hungry predators all the time. Their mission seems to be concentrated on scurrying ahead of annihilation, like pollen grains and plankton in the sea. This might also be said of us, except that we have grown into the business of inventing annihilation, outside of earth's constraints, and are more to be pitied than the voles.

The rain pours in from the south on a driving wind. Canvas and rigging slap hard on the sailboat moored offshore. The seas ride high beyond the headlands. There are no gulls in sight. All the world is commanded by the waters.

The Chinese poet Lao-tzu wrote of the wind and the tides which pour in with their periodic advents and departures, but what they measure is the immeasurable, the flow of eternity. This weather surrounds the globe. I am only a note taker of the immediate, trying to put down what strikes me as significant in my local world before it escapes me. I have spent too much of my life running after events, but they are fragmentary and elusive compared with the great sea, frightened with light, that pulls all things into its orbit.

The terms we use for things are only useful to me when I can incorporate them into myself, changing, as we all do, from year to year, growing past our insulation when we take our readings, and our headings, from every form of life that carries the future with it. When "diversity" is only used to count the numbers its meaning is hollow before it starts. We have run away from a real equation with the earth, inviting nowhere to come in.

An ecosystem does not thrive because we are capable of naming all its component parts, but because of its inner exchange between dissimilar forms of life. Our collaborators, often unacknowledged, are in the soil, the roots of plants and grasses, in the migrants of the living waters

and the air. What can we expect to accomplish
without them?

Autumnal changes, and the forms they take,
keep up a rhythmic pace which I sense even as
they leave me behind. I am always coming up on
things after the fact. Perhaps it is my own self-
consciousness that holds me back. But I stop
long enough to look at the leaf of a wild rose,
which has changed in my absence. It has turned
into a small, compact piece of tapestry, a sample
of subtle, evenly matched colors, blended to per-
fection. When leaf fall comes, it is not so much a
matter of falling out and dying, but an arrival.
One golden shower out of the sunlight, eddying
like small birds, falls in, to join the multifarious
communities that make up the ground.

I am timed by travelers beyond my sight, but
they come in out of darkness and distances to en-
courage me. By early September, the harbor seals
will have moved away to deeper waters off the
coastline. All summer, they choose periods of
high tide to haul out and lie on a tiny island of
rocks to sun themselves. On another, far side of
the cove, I look every year for a flock of black-
bellied plovers, primarily young, to roost temporarily along the rocky shore, after their nesting
season in the tundra. In some years, if only for a
day or two at the end of August, nighthawks fly
in to swoop and circle in the air hunting insects,

like greater swallows. Migrants from after, or nearby, like the crickets, or nuptial flights of ants, or the flowering of asters, combine to center us on an apex of the turning earth, and in ourselves we sense a better timing that finds us where we stand.

Watchers

The long stories of the world are still being played out in the labyrinths of the earth which are largely unexplored by those of us who only walk upon its surface. One day in October my daughter Susan and I were following a footpath above the sea at Maine's Reid State Park. We spotted a group of loons vigorously splashing, ducking in and feeding in the tidal current running by the shore. As we watched, a small animal suddenly materialized from behind the rocky ledges at our backs.

A head appeared, with a pair of big, intensely luminous dark eyes. Then it dropped out of sight, to reappear, having popped out of a crevice in the rock. ("Pop, goes the weasel.") It stood straight up in front of us, this little master, like the conductor of an orchestra, with a reddish brown jacket of fur and a white front, with a yellowish tinge to it, and looked at us boldly, uncompromisingly in the eye.

Away it went again ("Now you see me. Now

you don't."), scampering at a fast pace and disappearing into a narrow opening in the rock, then up again to view us, caution and speed in the same frame. It must be jealousy, in such heavy mammals as ourselves, which gave rise to such disparaging terms as "weasel words," or "slick as a weasel." Its bright intensity and boldness outlasts our epithets.

I once saw a fisher in a cage. It had been hit by a car and held for treatment. This is another fast animal living in forests where it can chase red squirrels from tree to tree, dashing over narrow, extending branches. I watched this one, a female, half grown, as she rushed back and forth inside the cage. How could a squirrel escape such a dynamo! Fishers, in some quarters, are not popular either, possibly because of their sharp little teeth and a reputation for ferocity. But how admirably animals are made in order to chase their own lives to the end of possibility.

Weasels hunt the prey down dark cracks and tunnels which are inaccessible to us, though we well remember the dark caves and corridors that attracted us when we were young. Children and weasels share in stories that go deep into the past, long before the application of rational knowledge. I would not give up watching a weasel, or having it watch me, for all the volumes of information about it that I can find.

This fierce little animal, with its earth colors soon to turn white as winter's snow, brought its curious audacity to the surface. It seemed to defy all the clumsy questions that rose in my mind about its nature and its habitat. Its secrets were almost nontransferable. In its brief revelation of a hidden life of caution, constant risk, and savagery, it was very real, but the fantasy and shadow of stories endlessly repeated came with it too. An encounter with a weasel reveals a past we can never really leave behind.

Our remote ancestors, as Stephen Potter and Laurens Sargent pointed out in their book called *Pedigree: Words from Nature,* were above all practical and realistic. "It is of supreme importance," they say, "in any enquiry into the origin of a name that what counts most among primitive people is activity, not appearance. Colour, size and other physical characteristics are incidental; behaviour is all important.

"The more man has to battle against Nature, the more utilitarian and practical will be his outlook . . ."

In other words, our human ancestors took more notice of the shriek of a bird which disturbed their hunting than they did of its plumage, but the mysteries behind inescapable nature were never alien.

Again from Potter and Sargent:

Anyone who ponders on the evolution of the concept of Nature as reflected in our language is made to realize again and again that the thought of Nature as something to be enjoyed for its own sake did not exist in the minds of our ancestors. They wondered about it continually. They were obsessed by the mystery of the sun, moon, and stars. They were closely concerned with flowers and trees. They were always, like the Oldest Inhabitant, talking about the seasons and the weather. But their way of expressing their wonder might be to propitiate the god of storms by dedicating a field to his name; or to pick a bunch of Prunella because the leaves of the purple-flowered plant might cure headache or boils; or to work out a horoscope favourable to a fertile marriage between the farm-cow and the town-bull.[1]

Some of these observations may not seem too remote to the family farm, as we used to know it, where the practical side of things far outweighed the mysterious. Your average farmer never did care very much for pests and "varmints." To subdue the wild, or the "Mother Nature" it represented, meant much more to most of them than did accommodation. The farmer controlled

1. Stephen Potter and Laurens Sargent, *Pedigree: Words from Nature* (London: Collins, 1973).

his stock. A bull that ran amuck could not be tolerated.

Primitive is a term of convenience, used to describe less developed and less complex organisms on the evolutionary ladder, or it refers to human societies we think are less advanced than we are. Still, what could be more dangerous and backward than a whole world isolating itself from the rest of creation through a false assumption of superiority? It has become easy for us in the modern world to substitute ideas of ownership for a wilderness that was never owned except by original life, in immense variety. To live with it was both extremely dangerous and exalting, and some of those distant ancestors of ours, on the near edge of the unknown, translated their whole experience into unforgettable art.

Who could look at the drawings, carvings, and paintings on the cave walls of France and Spain, twenty to thirty thousand years old, without marveling at their artistry? They reflect a close and passionate engagement with a world of primal life. Those shaggy mammoths and bisons, those bellowing bulls, the wild horses with beautifully shaped heads, galloping or entering a river, the deer, the great bear, the salmon, and the birds, are eternally present. Onlookers from a vast distance, we are brought in to see an uncompromised equation of a hunting people with the great animals that shared their world, and measured their destiny. So the hunter-artists carried their torches in to light a reverential darkness.

When I was teaching at Dartmouth College in New Hampshire, Professor E. O. Wilson, the distinguished Harvard biologist, came to lecture in the biology building. His subject was insects, primarily flies. Two friends of mine on the faculty of the English department declined to come when I suggested it, on the grounds that it would be a lowering experience. On the basis of Wilson's reputation as an exponent of altruism and cooperative behavior in animal communities, they seemed to be afraid, as Robert Frost put it in *The White-tailed Hornet,* of "instituting downward comparisons." I remember thinking that those who neglect the subterranean may find themselves gasping at high altitude in thin air. As Carl Jung expressed it: "Innovations come from below."

On these late fall mornings in Maine, all the waters surrounding us are full of waiting, and there is a misty silence hanging in the pines. The days, weeks, and months go by with increasing speed, so that when at last I try to put the fragments down in writing, I find myself a year, or years, behind, back in some irretrievable autumn in the past. A great blue heron stands in the shallows at low tide ready to stab a minnow or a crab.

At times, a male heron may stay too long, apparently so fixed or bonded to its own feeding territory, zealously guarding against intruders, that it fails to migrate. Winter comes in hard, covering the food supply with ice and sporadic snow, and the bird begins to starve to death. Although the heron may seem more rigid than we are, at our frenetic pace, it is not so much that they are relics of an age of dinosaurs, with their long necks and their glaring eyes. They are more like traditionalists of long standing. An insistence on territory, sensing enough of the watery world as to be able to return to the right place, even to risk standing still forever, is a principle of survival. For that we ought to welcome heron, as enduring landmarks. As a multiple, managed society, our actions often have unforseeable results. A heron may seem more rigid, less adaptable than we are. At the same time, if what it counts on is a lasting prehistoric containment, it may be wiser than we are in the long run.

It is by sharing the sight of others that we extend our own vision into our surroundings. Without their aid and company, we are in danger of only seeing a man-made wall and a flickering screen. One night, I walked out cautiously below the house, pushing one foot in front of the other, while holding a flashlight in my hand, and listening to the soughing of a light wind in the trees. Ahead of me I saw two eyes reflected in my light that met mine with an electric fire. It might have been a coon, like the one I once caught raiding the henhouse, or perhaps our fox, whose eyes, I am told, may shine red in a car's headlights. Foxes have eyes similar to a cat's, another nocturnal predator. Their pupils dilate elliptically, up and down, rather than in a round fashion like a dog's. The highly specialized eyes of lynx, a brilliant yellow-gold in color, have a powerful ability to retain all possible light in the dark of night. Its name derives from the Greek, *lugx,* which became *lux* in Latin, and our *light.*

Earth watchers, with an astonishing variety of components and abilities, are in the grasses and in the soil beneath them. We share our sight too, with newts, salamanders, frogs, and fishes, in the searching earth in every degree between dry and wet surroundings. Seeing through, which the human mind counts on for insight, clarity, and deliverance, is innate in the common conduct of life on the planet.

A fishy eye implies something leaden, opaque, with no life to it, and that is the way many people now think of fish, being exposed to little more than the reduced supply lying in icy silence on the market shelves. Yet the sight of fishes is integral with the brilliance and changing of all the waters, from shallow inland streams to the graduating depths of the ocean. With their large, round eyes, deep sea fishes are capable of seeing at over a thousand meters below the surface. They can also register small, bioluminescent sparks in the water. Not sight alone, but bodily senses make fish societies acutely aware of their location in the water systems where they swim, as well as the close presence of others in any given school.

Without the inner direction-finding of a bird, we follow the main road south, the big trail that crosses over and preempts all other tracks and trails, and we get there fast. The twentieth century has made it possible to overcome any intervening distance, at any appropriate speed. At the same time it has erased consecutive time. It becomes much harder to recognize the original inhabitants.

On our way, the gulls, herring or black-back, drift in from the ocean shore, gleaming white under the sky, and disappear. They are our camp followers, having taken advantage of modern growth and waste to greatly increase their population. Hundreds of thousands of gulls, following offshore fishing fleets and urban sprawl, have succeeded a relative few that once occupied a limited range of the coastal North Atlantic. For the most part, we take gulls for granted, except when they overcrowd refuse heaps or dispossess their smaller cousins the terns from their nesting islands. During the course of my lifetime, I have seen at least a few of them on an almost daily basis. The times of the year when they are most abundant always have to do with their discovery of new sources of food. In April, thousands crowd the mouth of the local creek at the time when the alewives swim in from the sea. One wonders how long their population can hold up in the face of our devastating assaults on the great marine ecosystem. Still the long enduring cycles of plenty or near starvation are so built into natural systems that gulls might be able to endure more successfully than we who pretend to be independent of them. It is a constant habit with these practical birds to keep looking out beyond the immediate. Their wing beat accommodates the enduring tides.

How can I tell you how much I have learned from the gulls, after putting them down for so many years as mere hangers-on and scavengers? They have taken me halfway around the coastal ranges of the planet which they occupy with such assurance. Their various races, each distinct in terms of where it lives, ranging from the light and dainty, to the large and bold, such as our great black-backed gull, shine with the brilliant capacity of the seas.

The big heavy-bodied glaucous gull, of all white or very pale gray plumage, derives its name through Latin from the original Greek *glaukos,* shining or gleaming, which also suggests the iridescent blue green, or blue gray, of the sea, colors familiar to horizon watchers all over the world. This shining name for a glaucous gull may also have had some root in the fact that it has translucent feathers on the tips of its primary feathers — but all our local gulls, as well as their small, far-ranging cousins, shine like the white caps on the waves and the ever dominating sky.

What strikes me most directly about the herring gulls, for example, is not the behavioral game they share with us in their aggressiveness and built-in evasive reactions to threats. We seldom give them much credit for mutual sympathy. What affinity they may have for each other seems to be no more remarkable than the cohesion of a school of fish. But I remember what I saw one October day, when I was walking along Cape Cod's Nauset Beach, that altered my opinion. I had passed a young black-backed gull which was sitting on the sand and failed to react to me, giving the impression that it was sick or injured. On my way back from the point where the beach is bisected by the tidal channel coming out of Nauset Marsh, I noticed that the bird had not moved, though it was still alive. Then another gull, of the same age, flew in to land next to the other, but on one leg. The other leg was dangling from its body. It moved in close and got no reaction, as if the two birds knew each other, possibly because they had come from the same nest and had suffered a common calamity. Whatever the reasons behind their behavior may have been, they obviously had an unshakable, close affinity for each other. As an ignorant bystander from an alien race, I felt very sad for them all the same. We can never begin to see into other forms of life without compassion. The savage and pitiless encounters we often associate with nature are not a fraction as dangerous as our modern efforts to eliminate them, in the name of an order exclusive to our own species. Without some admission of love, we will always be outsiders, judging other forms of life as if they could have no analogy to our own, and all the lessons of ethnology are to no avail.

Windows on Space

Sitting out during the noon hour, under the wide skies of Maine, we have often watched the vapor trails of passenger jets as they come in from Europe. As the planes move west or south, on time, heading on straight trajectories for their destinations, these trails, broad white woolly bands, begin to fray, to curl at the edges and disappear as the planes pass over. The passage across the Atlantic once took months, instead of hours, over monotonous or turbulent seas; it was hazardous, never "convenient," and the sea often took its toll of lives. At the same time, the world ocean was the major confluence of all travel and exploration. We can now cross all time zones and navigate the globe, thirty thousand feet or more in the sky, while being abstracted from our surroundings. The passengers sit in their cramped seats waiting for the landing, the passive spectators of our age. We soon land back home again, with its speeding machines, having crossed the globe with impunity. Distance and time have been almost fused together.

Our age, measuring time in milliseconds or millions of years, can reverse it, or change it to match our needs. The Hubble telescope can now peer into space far beyond what any previous telescope has been able to do. Behind our own galaxy are trillions of stars, always out of reach. The astronomers can peer off, millions of light years into space, toward the big bang, and the presumed origin of the universe. It must be where Nowhere begins, and one might wonder what we will know, or do, when we get there. The human race has never progressed so far without imagining that it would be possible to return. We exist, after all, within an inheritance of light, and our co-inheritors are endlessly resourceful in their use of it. The conquest of time and space is only an empty phrase without the inclusion of life itself, the real fire in our small corner of the universe.

A calendar is empty of all but numbers if it leaves no room for the arrival and departure of distinguished visitors, nonhuman as well as human. One day, as I was walking along the shore, I saw four large birds which I had never, to my knowledge, seen before. They came swinging in together on strong wings beautifully synchro-

nized, flying low over the sparkling waters. I recognized them as cormorants, part of a major
company of fishing birds. A smaller relative, the
double-crested cormorant, breeds on outer islands on the outer shores, and can be seen shut-
tling back and forth all summer long, settling on
the water, curving over and diving in after small
fish. These great cormorants, as they turned out
to be, were about the size of a snow goose. They
flew past me, then turned to land on a high
rock protruding above the running tide. As they
flew by me, I saw a bluish green luster on their
black feathers. When they landed they had a very
straight, upright carriage, and a look of proud,
professional competence, like a squad of skilled
professionals brought in to handle a special task.
Their powerful hooked bills seized fish as they
swam after them under water with great speed.
Their abilities have long been employed in the
Far East by fishermen who train them to go after
fish and to return with the catch.

The great cormorants soon left our shore and,
with their look of authority, flew off together
as one flock, heading south toward the mid-
Atlantic states where many of them winter. They
had flown from nesting grounds on rocky cliffs
or on isolated ledges to the north of us. Their
original range stretched all the way from Greenland to the Maritime Provinces of Canada. Some

still nest in Maine's Penobscot Bay; great cormorants are in fact the one of the dominant species during the winter time. If we were to think, as we seldom do, in terms of whole communities, of birds as well as men, the implications might become more clear. The more such birds, like our own native fishing people, begin to disappear, the more isolated we become from native competence, and from the real sense of the worlds of life that surround us. If you are unable to see a great cormorant in terms of an ancient and indispensable authority, the essential links between us begin to disappear, and in our detached state we become too ignorant to restore them.

The season in these latitudes does not move out or migrate to distant places like migrant birds; it changes form and color, like all other seasons, in response to the incontestable dictates of the sun. We see a new wind, new rain, and the clouds changing shape and momentum as they float in the clear sky with the pace of all the summers.

The sea calls me out. My own errands and routine seem unbearably confining. I would travel with cormorants, those professionals of all fishing expeditions. I wait on the spiders which make funnel-shaped webs in the grass, spangled in early morning with drops of dew. I do not know enough about how they live and what their mysteries are. I would be carried on a wind which is free of possession, leading me through the steadfast trees. I am interested in moving with the mind of birds. I do not take our word for it that this is not worth investigating. I feel the inner need to follow water channels in all their complex association. I want to be freed from the assumption that we can carry the world on our shoulders. We have never conquered the exactions of life's real journeys. I know this through watching the plants, feeling eel grass streaming out again with the ebbing tide. Nothing is more restricting than our abstention. Real freedom lies in participation with what lies beyond conquest or control. I live for another season when the fireflies carry me over the fields and rise toward the heights of the trees. I must always be on the alert for the unexpected, and for new neighbors I have never known before.

On the far side of the road that passes our house and leads to the town landing is an area of swampy land, full of rivulets after snowmelt or heavy rain; they are covered with dense undergrowth and close-growing trees. New owners had purchased the land on one side of the road, and were constructing an access road. Walking down it with a friend one day, we picked up two small, faded, rounded wings from the dirt thrown up by the bulldozer. They were partially spotted with white, and I recognized them as belonging to a small owl, which had probably lost its life a long time since. The only resident owl species it was likely to be was the northern saw-whet, a name derived from its call, which sounds like a saw being sharpened with a file. This tiny owl inhabits coniferous forests with densely growing trees. The saw-whet may roost during the day near its nesting hole, but it is strictly nocturnal, hunting mice; it will also prey on some insects. This was a resident, only a few hundred yards away from our house, which I had never seen before.

I had seldom walked through the land the owl had chosen to live in, partly because of its mosquitoes. It is not the kind of area that most home owners would value very much, unless it could be filled in. The saw-whet had a better idea of what it was worth, having a more intimate and useful sense of what it offered. That perfect little bird, with its great round, yellow eyes, is able to see in poor, or half-light which makes it capable of making the best use of its surroundings. Such sight, and its special discrimination, illuminates the small corner of the land it inhabits.

On the other side of this continent, in the great, old growth forests of the Northwest, is a similar species, the spotted owl, which was all we had to slow down the destruction of the trees and the export of their lumber. It was hung in effigy. Short-term profit has poor eyes to see with. The question of which of us, owls or men, is the most restricted is open to interpretation. Worlds cleared of trees and birds are replaced by another, blazing with artificial light; a world that can turn night into day, to the extent that we can hardly tell one from the other. The modern world, at its distance, is capable of flattening whole landscapes simply because it has the mechanical ability to do so. Yet the still enduring landscapes are held together by the sight and senses of the lives that really occupy them.

It is with the eyes of others that I see—cormorants or harbor seal, silvery herring, the rippled green, black, and yellow body of a mackerel slipping through the sea, newt, frog, or fly, the turtle with its yellow eyes descended from the sun. We can all become seers in their company.

Tern Islands

By late August, the swallow talk, or collo-quium that reflects the underlying unity of the young and the adults, diminished, but I can still hear what I call "lofty talk" coming from a few remaining corners of the barn. One parent flies in to quickly feed its young, then almost immediately flies out again with a short cry of alarm, as I enter the barn. Having listened to the swallows' "vocalizing" for many years, I am unable to put it down as nothing but bird talk. Like much of swallow behavior, it amounts to communication pared down to essentials; it comes out of fundamental expression and feeling following millenniums of disciplined migration. All of our trained observation, our naming and listening, must fail to give this speech the elevated status it deserves.

I am always surprised, no matter how many times it has been repeated, by the shortness and intensity of a season of nesting birds. Courting, nesting, brooding, and rearing chicks is accomplished with such dispatch, flying through all accidents and disasters, that it might look like "short lives making short work of it." But the swallows' performance during this vital season is never hasty. Theirs is a ceremonial with an earth experience and rhythmic consistency behind it. When the swallows leave, they carry the great principles of space on their wings.

I attended a conference in mid-August at the Maine Audubon Camp on Hog Island. Its purpose was to review the summer's work, of interns and ornithologists, at various managed tern colonies between Maine and Canada, and to the south along the New England coastline. Originally, before the settlers from Europe moved in, there were hundreds of thousands of terns nesting on Maine islands every year. In 1885 common and arctic terns occupied some seventy-five islands in the state, but in a few years so many of the birds had been slaughtered for the millinery trade, to adorn women's hats, that their colonies were reduced by 50 percent. At the beginning of this century there were only sixteen nesting islands left. Market gunners were also destroying shorebirds at a terrible rate, and one of them, the Eskimo curlew, was driven into extinction.

Terns and a number of shorebirds began to make a slow comeback after the relentless and murderous waves that faced them were partially held back by legislation. During this century the gulls, benefiting from the massively growing waste that accompanied the rise of industry and the cities, proved to be another serious threat to the terns, preying on their eggs and young. The terns have been forced out of many islands both by the gulls and by a relatively uncontrolled human presence. The islands remaining to them through conservation must be carefully monitored to keep them safe. Both terns and shorebirds are vital links to the lifelines of the continent. It must follow to all but the most removed of us that a seabird's life has a direct correlation with the living food of the seas. The state of one reflects the state of the other.

There were about forty people at the tern conference on Hog Island, seated on metal chairs in a wide circle under the shade of the trees. As the sun changed position during the morning and afternoon, many people were forced to keep moving their chairs so as to escape its glare. I thought of schools of small fish along the shore, slowly moving in response to changing light and shadow. We can never escape the sun's authority.

Each participant in turn reported the summer's progress at individual islands. As I listened, each person in turn giving an account of the terns' daily, weekly progress on his or her island, I noticed that no one argued about conclusions. They were all concentrating on the observed world of other creatures that had become, to a varying degree, almost unstated extensions of

themselves. We can close the inevitable gap between us and the birds through close attention to
the spheres of life they occupy, as part of a great
geography of changing shores. Any one of those
individuals, though they might be deeply trou-
bled or angered by the times that were thrust
upon them without their own volition, could
convey their hope or deep concern through the
information they were reporting; no one was indifferent. Implicit in their statements, aside from
facts and figures, was a recognition that though
seabird and human beings never shared a rational kingdom they were equal in a common sea.
The future becomes more possible when we are
not confined to our own vision of authority. I
suspect that not all tern watchers are inclined to
see God in their own exclusive image.

I watched and followed those black-capped,
fork-tailed "sea swallows" for many years. They
were my instructors, making up for a failed education. It was too late for me to contribute anything new to science, but I saw in them a true image of all the seas they traveled in, to which they
brought all their innate domesticity and fire. I
first began to pay attention to terns when I saw a
small flock one autumn day, as it gathered on the
sandy bands of an inlet off Cape Cod Bay. One of
them was feeding another, but this was not part
of a courtship ritual in the spring. It then dawned
on me, because its head lacked a black cap, that

this was a juvenile being fed small fish by its parent. I began to see how their form and behavior, their inborn skills made them superb practitioners of that great tidal sea to which they were born.

The terns were always as practical in their ways as any fishing people, now too often overcome by a run ahead to technology which is indifferent to its own effects. They have been sadly reduced in numbers, and their islands isolated from each other. I remember a wonderful trip to an island called Laeso, lying in shallow seas off northern Denmark. On one side of the island were grassy inlets like stepping stones, one beyond the other, and in between them rocks stood out like minor megaliths. With an ornithologist from the Copenhagen Museum of Natural History, I walked for hours through low water, hardly noticing its tidal rise and fall. It was in the full month of June, and the islets were full of breeding birds.

As I wrote about it afterwards:

Of the terns there were the Sandwich, a few Gull-billed, and a scattering of the Arctic and the Common. The region also had Oystercatchers, European Avocets, shelducks, and eiders, Common and Black-headed Gulls, each kind on its chosen nesting and feeding grounds—grassy, sandy, or stony, on bank or flat—with some, like the Gull-billed Tern, showing a preference for lower, wetter places. The Sandwich Terns nested here in close flocks, grouped in two main areas, and when disturbed they rose in a concentrated mass of beating white and silver wings, making a canopy overhead. Common Terns were few in number, with scattered nests on smaller islets. The Arctics were also scattered in small groups, over grassy meadows closer to shore. I caught sight of one of their half-grown, blue-gray chicks as it moved away to hide in the grass. In other parts of Europe where the populations of the two species are dense, they are sometimes more closely associated.

The Gull-bills feed more on insects than on fish, though they eat freshwater animals such as frogs, and are often found near inland ponds and marshes. In Europe they occur more commonly in latitudes to the south of Denmark. This colony was at the northernmost limit of their range, and was probably a remnant one, barely hanging on. The terns had been disturbed recently by local picnickers, whose children had taken the eggs and thrown them around, or enjoyed themselves shifting them from one nest to another. This had caused one of the two groups of Sandwich Terns to desert their nests and try again on another little island not far from the first.

I had begun to learn some of the differences among species of terns, variations on the ancestral theme: size and color, length of tail, shape of bill and wings, and specialized physical characteristics became clearer to me; but what really struck me as we wandered on, surrounded by terns flying, flocking, and sitting on their nests, not to mention other species of birds, was the depth of associated life that I began to feel around me.

Terns with high trilling laughs, such as the Gull-billed, Sandwich terns sounding a little like frogs with their occasional "Rek-rek," terns rising all at once, or singly, or which brooded unseen on their nests in the grass, took part in an intricate web of response. I sensed a timing, unknown to me, in all the birds that moved or raised their wings as I passed. I guessed at unknown ranges of signaling between them. I felt a continual testing out by them of their surroundings. This low-lying seaside land was their intimate, and who knows how they responded to all its changes?

On still another side of the island, where we walked the following day, there was a wide beach. Ridges of sand had been pushed in to the head of the beach by storm tides, and behind that lay a gray swale of pebbly and sandy ground and then a stretch of small rippling dunes held down by beach grass. We came there to look for Least Terns. Watching from the dunes, we finally saw two pairs settling down in a pebbly area and we walked out to look for the eggs, while the birds dipped back and forth over our heads, with cries of alarm. Having located one nest with eggs in it, I walked away and barely avoided stepping on another one, in which there was a newly hatched chick, a mere flicker of yellow on the ground, that might have been a chip of wood or a bunch of dried grass. It was not much over two inches long, with fine dark tracings on its tiny back, of a beige color, tinted with honey from the sunlight. The chick seemed completely helpless and unprotected on that bare ground, and I might have feared for it; but its parents were ardent in its protection, and I knew that an exposure that looked perilous to a man meant all that was reliable to a tern.

As we walked back in the late afternoon across shortgrass meadows, called "Strand Eng" by the Danes, Oystercatchers were crying out noisily and monotonously, "Kteep! Kteep! Kteep!" An avocet with broad wings and showy black and white plumage did a broken-wing act to lead us away from its nest—it almost seemed to know what a striking effect it had. Who could help being distracted by such a display! A dark kestrel suddenly swooped down toward a nestling in the grass, and a pair of Arctic Terns shot up, crying harshly, and drove it away. A pair of Turnstones stood stolidly out in the open, but with a look of extreme alertness. I had the feeling of watchful eyes and senses everywhere. The place was full of guardians, sentinels, and protectors. So while the birds gave their papertearing, shrill, or whistling cries, we left the Strand Eng, grass woven, sea fibered, behind, waiting for the wild and ancient, copper-tinged twilight to come in.[1]

When our world thinks of animal communities, or "wildlife," it is inclined to set them apart, perhaps as an unconscious reaction to danger. We remove what might harm us. The conscious terms we use for these other worlds, such as wildlife itself, or "creatures," often strange and exotic, of an "environment" tend to remove the image from its reality. And even such often-used terms as *ecology,* even *nature* itself, begin to lose substance and real meaning. In a sense, the animals are subordinated to a mythical assumption of human mastery, though we disprove it every day. It is as if we were territorially minded animals forced to destroy our own territory. We lose what many now mourn as a "sense of place" because we cast ourselves adrift from the essence of any place, created by all the life that it is composed of.

When I walked away from the highly alive and watchful shores of the Strand Eng, I had the feeling of being brought into an ancient land whose lineage, from time out of mind, was being expressed by all the life around me. No one

1. John Hay, *Spirit of Survival* (New York: E. P. Dutton & Co., 1974).

race presided over any other. A greater history brought predator and prey together, thriving on the edge of hunger, danger, and vitality. The northern sea, stretching off toward undiscovered worlds, contained all history, and was still life's ultimate provenance and shelter. All the local and disparate forms of life were held together, not only in a coexistent, but a coeternal community.

The terns' exposure to the weather is constant. Along sandy shores, early spring storms may inundate low-lying nests, or bury eggs and chicks in wind-driven sand. The parents are intensely engaged in brooding and rearing their young, and always on the alert for predators. Fog and rain may hold back their fishing flights; extreme heat can kill featherless chicks. Even the arrival of a thunderstorm can be an unnerving event, especially after dark. At times, and for no apparent reason, they may engage in a "dread flight," silently flocking up from their nests and flying over the water. They are born of an elemental weather, and behave that way. While we can never entirely escape the more violent forms of the global weather, such as hurricanes, typhoons, drought, fire, and blistering heat, we do everything in our power to avoid them. The myth of protection against nature has carried us a long ways, even to the extent of trying to dispense with it. But these endlessly responsive birds are inseparable from the great earth designs that send them out. They act within the constraints and allowances of the life-sustaining sea.

Several years ago, I took a two-day trip conducted by the Maine Audubon Society to Passamaquoddy Bay; it was in late summer. Out boat passed the town of Eastport. Old brick row houses lined the banks as we headed out. Their windows were boarded up, all along a waterfront that was once a thriving center for the fisheries. We moved out over swirling waters, with twenty-foot tides, which were rich at this time of the year in copepoda and the krill that fed on them. This rich source was fed on in turn by phalaropes, said to number in the hundreds of thousands in late August and September, a pivotal time in the year. Terns, after the nesting season and before their fall migration, also fed over these waters. All along the rocky headlands were the ever-present gulls, standing out like sentinels, crying out in stentorian tones. We passed two bald eagles roosting in spruce trees that rose out of an island lodged on massive building blocks of rock that lined the shore. The great birds showed woody brown feathers against the deep green shadows of the spruce around them. They seemed as majestic and powerful as the

shores that bore the weight of all the waters. Beyond the islands, enormous finback whales were
blowing, over a wide area, each with an explo-
sive "whoosh." They glided through the water
and then dove under the surface with gracefully
arched backs, their great fins raking behind
them, hunting fishes in the depths.

Machias Seal Island, across the boundary line
between the United States and Canada, had a
population, at that time, of two hundred pairs of
common terns and twenty-six hundred arctics.
As we left the boat and climbed ashore, we saw
hundreds of them, their white and gray bodies
covering the dark, slippery beds of seaweed that
clothed the rocky flanks of the island. The thin,
reedy cries of the arctics contrasted with the distinct calls of two other seabird species nesting
on the island. Groups of razorbill auks had gar-
gling voices, and the puffins made low, mooing
sounds, with the harsh quality of a chain saw.
The terns had made their nesting scapes in the
spring when the ground was relatively bare, but
now heavy vegetation covered the island with
dock, angelica, and other plants which benefit
from the annual droppings of generations of seabirds.

Later on, walking on the gray, stony shores
of Passamaquoddy, on a narrow stretch of beach
at high tide, I met a flock of a thousand or

more semipalmated plovers, stopping by on their southerly migration. From a distance, they looked like so many stones themselves, covering the narrow beach. Suddenly, they all rose into the air at once, sweeping out low over the water, then whizzing back to land again, their white bellies shining in the light.

I will never forget the sunset off Quoddy, as it weighed in over a heavy, mercurial sea, all leaden and silver in the dying light. Its last, fading brilliance reflected a silvery flashing in the water, like those young herring, or "brit," wear on their sides.

The clouds in growing darkness carried smoldering fires and smoke from the sun as it passed off the ocean, signaling the inclusion of all life in these imponderable depths. I now think of those seabrids poised for migration, with great distances in their minds, as being as masterful in their style and endurance as any of the achievements of civilization. They were principal actors on the earth's great stage. We ourselves are distinguished not by what we are able to overrule, but by what we are a part of.

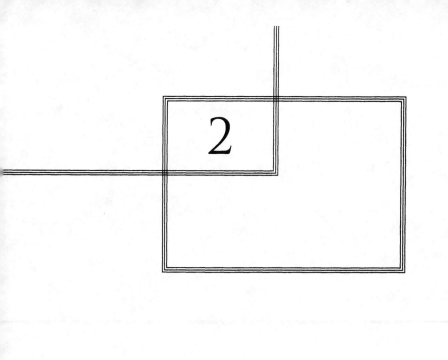

A Loss of Neighbors

W hen I first moved to Cape Cod after the close of World War II, I was at first not quite sure of why I did it. Should I not be attending to the world's business, as some friends suggested, instead of being holed up in the countryside? But a war that had turned the world upside down had cornered me and narrowed my range of choice. I was inwardly impatient for a scope and space that was being denied me. Europe's "dark night of the soul" had destroyed all certainty, tearing away millions of people from their attachments. When it was all over, I looked for signs of permanence, not of our own manufacture, but as ordained by the earth and the sun itself.

We moved into our newly built house in the autumn of 1946, and one of our first heart-lifting experiences there came from a flock of Canada geese flying past an open window. I learned that many of them had taken on the role of lazy scavengers, hanging out on the golf courses and polluting the greens, but that meant nothing to us who associated their triumphant bugling with the open skies of America.

I had purchased our acres, locally known as Dry Hill, for twenty-five dollars each, from Franklin Ellis, an old native who lived a few houses away from Conrad Aiken, the poet, and his wife Mary, the artist, whom I had stayed with before the war. The land was on the edge of a sparsely populated, backwoods section of town known as the Punkhorn. The name persists, in spite of the disappearance of many once-familiar place-names throughout the Cape, but I do not know its original meaning. Near our house is a well-worn path which, we were told, was named after one Ann Thankful Sears. It is quite possible that the name Ann might really have been Aunt, since Aunt and Uncle were commonly used in addressing people in the last century. Her path in any case still leads through a stretch of broken, spindly trees, held back by abused and disturbed soil, and periodic infestations of gypsy moths, not to mention hurricane winds bearing salt spray across the Cape.

The path leads to a cleared area, now being developed, but occupied when we arrived by a truck garden growing turnips and strawberries in sandy soil. Beyond it were a few small cottages and a gray weather-beaten house owned by a man named Bill Perry. In his vicinity there also lived a woman named Geneva Cash, one of the people imported from the Azores to pick cranberries at low wages.

On my walks in that direction, I sometimes stopped by to share the time of day with Bill Perry. We shared a common interest in his pigeons, which I had also kept as a boy in New Hampshire.

In a sense I have been walking backwards since we first moved here, looking over my shoulder at a receding past. Local history and its people started to go long before we arrived. The process only accelerated as time went on, part of the American habit of dispossessing, and then having to recreate, its own history.

The New England colonists had set to work cutting down the trees as soon as they landed on these shores. Photographs of Cape Cod during the late nineteenth and early twentieth centuries show a bare land, stripped of trees which were used for firewood, tryworks for whales, building material, and a hundred other things. Lumber became so scarce that it began to be imported from Maine. Still, local life developed through what poor-soil agriculture was able to produce; and more abundant food came from the long shore and the surrounding seas. Village life and rooted family ties barely survived the disruptions and encroachments of the outside world; they began to slip away like a man losing his grasp of a rope tied to a speeding boat.

One of our neighbors was a man by the name of Nate Black. When I needed to have my hair cut, I only had to walk down to the dirt road where his house and barbershop were located to have him do it. The sense of peace and stability it gave me lies in me still; and here is what I wrote about him during that period.

It seems to me that as the world has grown outward in recent years, even I, a comparative newcomer to Cape Cod, have lost some local life to memory. When you live in a place for the first time you see behind it to its roots and grain, before the storms of circumstance blow you away from it. I remember a few old men who seemed so representative of the old Cape that it will never be the same now that they are gone. The loss is of a country speech, the flavor of a flesh and blood nurtured on locality. What has replaced them can be defined in terms of California as well as Cape Cod, which means no detriment to either, for what we are now obliged to consider is locality in a wider field. But those old men were born as we may not yet be born, sturdily, in custom and resignation.

Nathan Black died in October 1957, at the age

of ninety-two. He was born in 1865, the year Abraham Lincoln was assassinated. He was a near neighbor. His land abutted mine, and since he was the proprietor of the Black Hills Barber Shop, I could walk down through the woods to get my hair cut, for the price, in a trillion-dollar world, of fifty cents. He was a heavy man, with bright brown eyes, and a head of curly white hair. He fitted the open Cape Cod weather, or the weather fitted him. I am not sure of the distinction. Nearly ninety years of change, of natural cataclysm, of both peace and abysmal war in the human world, had left him in the same place, with the same measure, outwardly at least, of stability.

When he left his place, or the customary orbit of work and old friends that constituted his life, perhaps to drive out on a new highway or to the chain store, he may never have stopped being surprised. I remember his looking at me with a kind of amused questioning—but not alarm—and saying something about no one belonging here any more. The new population didn't quite make sense to him.

In the way of old countrymen who knew their boundaries, he was tough and unforgiving in his role as landowner. He had his rights, "By gawly!" and he would know when someone did him wrong. He held on hard, and I suspect there were neighbors who felt the possessiveness too strongly, but this being none of my business, I will go in and get my hair cut.

The shop, with a tool shed under the same roof, where "Nate" used to grind knives and axes, stood, and still stands, across the yard from the house where he was born. There are some other gray-shingled, outlying buildings on both sides of a dirt road that runs through scrubby woods and hollows, dry hills sloping down to marshy bottom land . . . wood-lot country. One December day I rapped at the door, and he put his jacket on and walked across the yard with me, where two white ducks were parading and some red chickens giving the frozen ground a going over. The old man bent down a little and spoke to his dog Bonnie, a cream-colored spaniel, which had just wagged up to him: "Did you get it?"

Then, to me: "I lost an egg. Picked up five eggs, out of the hen yard this mornin', and came back with four. Maybe there was a hole in these old pants of mine."

The barber shop was small, long and narrow, but he had a stove in there and kept it warm. There were some old magazines on a bench against the wall, with a black Homburg hat hanging on a peg. It had been given to him by an old customer, a wealthy man who had lived on the Cape during the summer and had come in to have his hair cut for many years before he died. There was a photograph on the wall of the two of them with an inscription underneath that read: "Established 1884. A satisfied customer is our best advertisement." They were standing out in front of the shop, smiling in the sun.

"Feller came here yesterday and I had to clip him in the kitchen. Shop was too cold," Nate said.

The calm of the place was comforting. It came, I suppose, from an acceptance that emanated from him, and brought in many old friends, who would sit down to say: "Nate, just thought I'd come over and pass the time of day."

Whatever he had to say about other people never left them without the honor of human circumstances. "Pretty close, he is," he would say with a little laugh, or "I guess he had a shade on" (a Cape Cod expression for being drunk). "Guess you can't hold on to nothin'," he said about some local theft, in a way that insisted on not being roused beyond necessity.

His origins were out of a kind of history of which there was very little left intact except himself. He once showed me a tintype of his mother, a handsome girl named Bridget Malady, who had emigrated from Ireland in 1862. His father, Timothy Black, was born in Yarmouth, on the Cape. At the age of ten he signed on as a cook aboard the packet which sailed between East Dennis and Boston, and seems to have spent a good deal of his life on intermittent voyages at sea. He was also in the butchering and slaughtering business with his two sons. In the autumn they used to butcher eighty-five hogs or more, at the rate of three a day. And in some rough but related way, Timothy Black started his son in the barbering business. Nate remembered how his father used to cut his hair in the kitchen, long before the Black Hills emporium was established: "I used to sit there while he was sort of pummeling at me on the back of the neck. By gol! I sure did cringe when he was chopping me with those women's scissors."

While I, seventy or eighty years later, was sitting in the barber's chair, getting more expert and calmer work done on me, I assembled a little of the past. In the nineteenth and early twentieth centuries an expedition to the post office or the store took up a large part of the day. That was the time when you could hitch the horse up to a post and stop for a long chat, "having the capacity to waste time" as I heard a Texan phrase it about some of his countrymen in the western part of the state. People walked between their houses—there are foot paths still showing—on barren hills. They had small herds of cows that foraged on the sloping fields. Families used to picnic together by the ponds, and there were barn dances on Saturday nights, which were sometimes the occasion for a rip-roaring fight. I have heard it said that Nate

Black was the strongest fighter in the region, when outraged beyond his normal patience, but he would reveal none of his prowess to me.

The Black family also held dances in their kitchen. The father of the house played the violin. On such occasions they would have plum porridge suppers, or they served crackers, milk, and raisins, and sometimes hulled corn.

He was of a piece with his surroundings. I think of many things he talked about while I was having my hair cut and they all meant the gray, sea-girded land, and a human closeness to it. I think of the deer that ate his beans, of his duck that was carried off by a fox, of foxes being reduced in population by the mange, of a watering place for horses by Cedar Pond in East Dennis (a beautiful pond with ranks of dark cedars backing it up, and now being encroached upon by house lots); and he talked about the big eels waiting to eat young herrin' (or alewives) at the mouth of a pond, and of sounding the depths of Round Pond here in West Brewster.

And then there was his dog which had to be chained up because it got so wildly excited chasing rabbits through the woods that it was constantly lost, having once been picked up nearly ten miles away; and the coon that climbed a tree after a hen; and his little granddaughter wanting to shine a flashlight through the window one night and take a picture of a coon she saw outdoors, because it was "such a pretty-looking animal."

There also come to mind the fishing boats all-over white with screaming gulls, that he once spoke about with real excitement, and, of course, the yearly work on his cranberry bogs . . . he and his tart and lively wife used to pick them together; and the shifting price of cranberries, and his wood lots, and who was after him to buy some of his land.

"Yes, yes," he would say, in the Cape Cod fashion, and always when a customer was leaving the shop: "Come, again."

His wife Emily died two years before him. Some time before that I stopped to talk with him when he was scything the family plot in Red Top Cemetery, which lies at the junction of two country roads, on a little hill or high knoll up in the sky and the ocean winds. He told me two women had come up one day while he was there and said: "What a nice place!" He and his wife are buried there, in a place which has no more permanence than any other, but for them and by them had the simple power of acquaintance.[1]

Although some people have tried to live the way they did, getting their food from the sea, and keeping their own hours, the older natives

1. John Hay, *Nature's Year* (Garden City, N.Y.: Doubleday, 1961).

have gone. It is harder to hear them now, in the tone and rhythm of the tides. The Cape Cod highway came in and bisected this narrow peninsula, cutting off older communities, and introducing a kind of crowded loneliness. Walking room is hard to find in a land once open from sea to sea. The space is occupied by a hodgepodge of developments where it is easy to be lost. Everyone is on wheels, headed for all the supermarkets that have starved out the country store. The capacity for taking time is being replaced by a race for instant communication, which may soon replace our need for articulate speech.

Another loss has had to do with what we call "wildlife," a neutral term if I have ever heard one; it disguises the reality that we, in our capacity to denude the planet, are of a wildness which is not only unsettling but incalculable.

Deer are still present in our woods, moving out of range of the hunters in the fall, keeping to an ancestral route away from the highways and the new building lots. They are more wary than they were in earlier years when they came out of a fringe of trees to graze on the small meadow below our house. The male ruffed grouse which used to drum in the spring on our newly built terrace wall, a proud symbol of wilderness America, is no longer to be found. The towhees, or ground robins—whisking around in the leaves, smartly flashing the white feathers in their tails—are scarcer these days. So is the wood thrush and its dappled breast. Listening for it on a late spring evening was our pride and joy. That little wood warbler the ovenbird, whose nest is hidden in the leaf litter, used to call "teacher, teacher, teacher" as it flitted through the lower branches of the trees; it too is now very scarce. And where are the whippoorwills, whose wild, shouting calls kept us awake on spring nights, turning the darkness into a magic sounding board for their intensity? They are all gone, and the chief reason for this lamentable disappearance has to do with rapid growth of suburbs, and its thousands of domestic cats: ground nesting birds are an easy prey. So we all start to become absentee owners, temporary residents of an exchangeable land. How can we find our way, without those winged guides and leaders that have sought out this land from every point in the compass? The "ancestors" left only a few cart tracks behind them to trace a past existence; even local place-names are almost rubbed out in memory. We keep looking for attachments, but we pass them by.

This land, of course, has been battered for centuries, not only by human occupancy, but by hurricane winds, and the encroachments of the North Atlantic storms all along its exposed shores. Whatever permanence it has lies in the power that has cut it down. The wide oceanic horizon which anyone can drive to, even for an hour, is the ultimate carrier, the great messenger of unseen distance.

Crossing the highway by foot, and walking over to the beach two miles away, I come into a country which is always new. At low tide, when the sandy flats lie open for miles, the surface is covered with tracks and winding, irregular trails, and pitted with holes that are erased by every tide. I never go there without feeling that the names we attach to all forms of life mean very little in themselves. We have to look behind the names, into a changing creation we can only begin to know. We go down to the sea to deliver us from our own impermanence. In the presence of eternal form, the classical shell of a surf clam, or of a passing gull, or the slick fronds of seaweed made to accommodate the constant waves. I can share in all the beginnings and endings we can never account for on our own. I can temporarily free myself from my own insularity, to find, as John Muir did, that "going out is really going in."

Power and Light

D uring my boyhood years, as I tried to assimilate what I was being told, I had the mistaken idea that electricity was invented by Thomas Alva Edison. That conception must have had a short run in my mind, especially after lightning hit the power line and the lights went out. Higher powers, once associated with the church, began to move into the realities of the surrounding world. The occasional thunderstorms I grew to know and respect during the summer months were wonderfully expressive of an electrical alliance between the sky and the land. They spoke with the voices of a continent, although, as Francis Parkman pointed out in *The Oregon Trail*, thunderstorms in the East were tame by comparison with those that exploded across the western plains.

Scarcely had night set in, when the tumult broke forth anew. The thunder here is not like the tame thunder of the Atlantic coast. Bursting with a terrific crash directly above our heads, it roared over the boundless waste of prairie, seeming to roll around the whole circle of the firmament with a peculiar and awful reverberation. The lightning flashed all night, playing with its livid glare upon the neighboring trees, revealing the vast expanse of the plain, and then leaving us shut in as if by a palpable wall of darkness.

It did not disturb us much. Now and then a peal awakened us, and made us conscious of the electric battle that was raging, and of the floods that dashed upon the stanch canvas over our heads. We lay upon indian-rubber cloths, placed between our blankets and the soil. For a while, they excluded the water to admiration; but when at length it accumulated and began to run over the edges, they served equally well to retain it, so that toward the end of the night we were unconsciously reposing in small pools of rain.[1]

I do not know the exact connections between lightning and the water in the sky, or which runs like veins through all the land. I have seen great trees in the forests of New Hampshire which were deeply scarred by lightning strikes. I know of one dead, scorched white pine, stripped of its bark, that is still standing near the shores of the lake I once lived on. It has a deep fissure run-

1. Francis Parkman, Jr., *The Oregon Trail* (New York: Penguin, 1982).

ning down the length of its trunk. That tree has reminded me more than once of the terrible wounds that are inflicted on us during the course of a war, living tissue burned beyond repair. General war spares little in its way, but lightning, it is said, seldom strikes in the same place twice.

A thunderstorm, discharging its lightning between the clouds and the ground, is an outward expression of innate power and magnitude. We tap it for the uses and transmission of electricity, but in one form or another this generative power exists in ancient harmony with the worlds of life that invade and surround us. There is electric fire in the eyes of an owl or a bobcat, it leaps with a fish climbing a falls, it signals to us in glowworms and fireflies. I feel it in the wind that shakes the light in the leaves, and it springs at me with every falling wave. Life contains an everlasting fire.

Last year, after our return to Cape Cod from Maine, we heard the news of "fox fire" in a big woodpile near our house. Four years previously, a hurricane roared in and leveled many of the oaks in the woods that surround us. They were not in good condition to begin with, very slow to mature, weakened by disease and decay, having been repeatedly cut over for firewood for several hundred years. A ground that is continually disturbed, on dry, sandy slopes overlooking the sea, is not likely to produce strong trees. Only in sheltered hollows do they grow to much height.

Since the 1940s when I bought this "worthless woodlot," given acreage is no longer valued in terms of its woodlots, since firewood is not a necessity. Boundaries are not decided on the basis of a stone wall, or an old tree, but on strict lines drawn by absentee calculators. Since the price of land has risen to astronomic heights, and taxes have also risen, few people can afford to own more than a small plot for their houses. To find original, open space, of the kind I used to wander over, you have to go to an outer beach or a conserved area of land. What open space is left is being covered over and exchanged beyond recognition. It is hard to know a land that is only valued as a medium of exchange, nor can we depend on it, but the fires of growth and decay still burn beyond our control.

Because of the logs that were taken from it, our woodpile has become semicircular in shape, like an amphitheater, meant for the performance of magic games. After dark, we have been able to see ghostly little clouds of light all over it, which came, as we found out the following morning, from clusters, or aggregates, of small mushrooms, of the kind that invade the trunks and tissue of already weakened trees. I had heard of "fox fire" in rotting wood, and was once startled to see a luminous toadstool at night on the lower slopes of a mountain in Costa Rica, but I was never aware of it so close at hand. At first, I had a hard time trying to identify the species of fungi, a light tan in color. After I had sent its photos out to several learned friends I found out that it was *Panellus stipticus*, known to some by the fanciful name of the luminescent Pan. It is related to *Armullariella mellea*, or "honey mushroom," whose fox fire emanates from its mycelium, not as in *Panellus* whose light shines from all its parts, especially on warm, rainy nights during late spring into the fall. So it has been quietly glowing among us unseen, until this gathering of logs from the fallen oaks. Its function, as a parasitic agent, is to break down decaying wood. In the process, it produces this strange luminosity. It is also a saprophyte, feeding off the tissues which it attacks. That puts it in the category of white Indian pipe, growing out of the damp woodland soil.

The authors of the *Encyclopedia of Mushrooms*, published in 1983, in trying to suggest a need for luminosity, come up with the following:

We can, at present, only guess at the biological significance, if any, of luminosity. It has been suggested that luminous fruiting bodies attract insects which aid in spore dispersal by carrying spores on their wings and bodies. However, in many fungi luminosity is especially well developed in young colonies and it is difficult to see what advantages this may have for dispersal, or indeed any other process. Furthermore, there is still some doubt as to how fungi emit light, though it is assumed that the same mechanism operates as occurs in the luminous bacteria, the glow-worms and the fire-flies.

In these a chemical called, appropriately, luciferin reacts with an enzyme, luciferase, which alters the form of this phosphate-rich compound and in the process light is emitted. The light produced by fungi behaves similarly to other light waves, in that it will not penetrate cardboard or other opaque materials. This is of interest in that the Stinkhorn (*Phallus impundicus*) also produces radiations, which though non-luminous, will penetrate through a cardboard box and activate a photographic plate contained inside.[2]

The woodpile has had a number of visitors, as well as occupants. Skunks have come by, looking for grubs. Rabbits have hopped in and away. It has seen red squirrels as well as gray, though the latter, better suited to suburban life, have driven most of the reds away. One evening, as it was

2. Colin Dickinson and John Lucas, eds., *The Encyclopedia of Mushrooms* (New York: Crescent Books, 1983).

growing dark, I glimpsed the thin body of a coyote quietly disappearing into the brush beyond it. The logs shelter several species of ants, and when I turned one over I found a little red-back salamander, a glistening, slippery looking creature with goggle eyes. During medieval times, there was a popular notion that salamanders were poisonous, though there was no proof of it, similar to the idea many people have about mushrooms, of any kind. But what really held the salamanders in the medieval mind was the belief that they could survive within a fire. It was also thought that they could put a fire out. Pliny reported that "this serpent is extremely cold," which is not far from the truth, so far as reptilian circulation is concerned. But Pliny must have known perfectly well that they could not survive fire. He burned one, to make medicine from its ashes. The salamander became a symbol, a way of expressing something else than what can be literally described. In his *Bestiary, A Book of Beasts*, T. H. White writes of St. Augustine's belief that it did not matter whether certain animals existed; what did matter was what they meant.

We know today that salamanders will hibernate in rotting wood, and will seek out damp, cool places to live in. But it takes a stretch for us in this age to bridge the gap between accurate descriptions of a salamander's habits and biological nature, and seeing it as a symbol, one associated in our minds with myth and superstition. Myth does not satisfy our nagging demand for exact proof.

The woodpile, before its logs are all used up for indoor fires, provides a temporary haven for many appropriate forms of life, like the ants in the soil underneath and the wood lice, or "armadillos," partial to damp places. It becomes an ecological community of its own. But the cold fire which has invaded the wood, through its fungi, gives it another mysterious quality. At the center of this fire, allied to water and light, is the salamander, still entitled, it seems to me, to its ancient reputation, a symbol of the imperishable, in the great design of life.

Bioluminescence, as it is now called, has been seen and marveled at past recorded history. It was written about by Aristotle, as well as Pliny, and is mentioned in the epic poem of *Beowulf.* Sir Francis Bacon was the first to carry out experiments with luminous wood, though the literature of the Elizabethan age is full of it.

Bacon remarks in the course of his studies that, ". . . glow worms have their shining while they live, or a little after; only scales of fish putrefied seem to be of the same nature with shining wood."

At one time some kinds of fungi were used as

tinder for kindling fires. The following is an account taken from a fascinating and neglected little book, *Fungi Folklore*:

> In the central Highlands of Scotland a fungus found on old birch trees was used to kindle the bonfires that were lit on the first of May until the middle of the eighteenth century. Frazer, in "The Golden Bough" describes these so called Beltane fires which are thought to have been directly derived from Druidical ceremonies, and like so many of these were always celebrated on hill tops. Special oatmeal cakes were baked on the fires and they ended with young people leaping thrice through the flames.

From the same source comes an equally arresting account of the direct use of luminous wood by people who had close experience of forest lands:

> Luminous wood has long been known by woodmen and forest workers. It was used by people in the far north for lighting their paths through the forest during the long winter nights, as Olaus Magnus related in 1652, saying that they placed pieces of rotten oak bark at certain intervals on the proposed route. He also tells us that they used it as a kind of "safety lamp" that by its light (rather than that of a burning torch) they may

with more safety enter places full of combustible material, such as winter barns full of harvest crops or hay.

Mordecai Cooke (1862) mentions that "in our schoolboy days we remember to have often carried home in our pockets a piece of 'touchwood' to be taken to bed with us on account of the little light that it afforded." And Mark Twain, in "The Adventures of Huckleberry Finn" mentions "rotten chunks that's called 'Foxfire' that just makes a soft kind of glow when you lay them in a dark place."[3]

Where is that luminous America we once met for the first time? We tear out the woods for our exchangeable dwellings, and for the strip malls, and out of our ignorance we extinguish the living fire.

I am always astonished, after long periods of time, to come upon phenomena of such significance in what I had passed by a hundred times without noticing. Blindness brings illusions of a self-sufficient world which can carry us through, but if we lose our common ties with original fires we invariably lose.

I have had to wait for fifty years to pass in order to bear witness to the staying power and

3. W. P. K. Findlay, *Fungi Folklore, Fiction and Fact* (London: Richmond, 1982).

longevity of the trees. Our worthless woodlot is being reclaimed by its legitimate ancestors. Otherwise, I might never have known that what looked like little more than a series of glacial hollows and sand dunes, with little on them but scrub oaks and a few fledgling pitch pines, could have been so transformed.

The oaks, no longer "scrub," useless for anything but a sporadic source of firewood, have grown so tall, so capacious in their foliage, that they hide the view of the sea, once wide and open from one side of the Cape to the other. The oaks tend to shade out the pitch pines which once seemed to be growing more rapidly, and to kill them off. I have long known that these lichen-spotted trees nurtured properties of light, but the detail largely escaped me. A fungus or a tree can tell you straight that there is always time ahead for revelation.

The October sunlight burns on the enameled surfaces of the oak leaves, and about five o'clock in the afternoon all the woods seem to be smoldering with fire. It is as if the oaks in their own, partly unaccountable relationship to the earth were providing me with a great deal more than a passing comparison with my own, limited age and theirs. This new height of trees, seen after a lifetime of living with them almost unconsciously, provides me with a kind of jumping off point for the future. Our respective life spans seem immaterial to me. It is not only that they are capable of living on and claiming their place long after I am gone, it is also that they provide us with their own standards of an earth time embodied in every living thing. The inclusion is what gives us the stature we might rightfully claim. When we cast ourselves aside from the common rights and intervals of passage, on its grand scale, we are ephemeral as a mayfly, and less enduring as a race.

When my wife and I moved in and built a house in the middle of this "worthless woodlot," I thought it would stay that way, a permanently wrecked, impoverished environment. Half the oaks were dead, though still standing, and you could push them over at will. That was before I, as a transient inhabitant of a reckless century, became aware of the subterranean tides that follow us from sea to sea. I can now see that woodlands which have not been constantly, relentlessly cut down, and in effect buried for centuries, are still responding to earth tides and the powers of the ground.

Fungi Folklore also tells me that luminosity has sometimes been seen in fallen leaves during the autumn. This is due to the presence of small, bell-shaped toadstools, which may glow for two weeks or more. One of them "has the charming

Latin name of *Mycena tintinabulum*." I never knew that when I was shuffling through the leaves in the fall I might be kicking up bells of light.

Fungi in early autumn, especially after rain, begin to move in the dark soil. The mushrooms last for a varying, often unpredictable length of time and then disappear. Lichen covers the trunks of the gray trees and the rocks, often growing so slowly that you are unaware of it. Some of the logs in the woodpile grow a fungi that looks like blue paint. Some are yellow, some orange. Fall color is not confined to leaves. So I begin to see that this "worthless woodlot" has had a highly distinctive growth which I largely ignored. To come in on a new place always implies that it may contain hidden treasures not easily apparent at first. What I never really anticipated was how such a neglected and abused land could harbor so much potential fire.

Out of the woodpile, in our supposedly rational age, superstition and fear, even the grounds for belief in ghosts, reappears. Ghostly fire in a group of mushrooms, like strange light emanating from a swamp, or a rotting fish, was the stuff of much early myth and superstition. It is easy to believe in ghosts, as children often do, in the absence of scientific truth and authority. Half the world does not dare pick up or taste a mushroom because, with some reason, you might be poisoned. The ghostly light becomes a fact, or could be, if we had it explained to us, but to think that there always has to be a reason to account for almost any phenomenon may stifle curiosity. It becomes easy to stay away from mushrooms—"better safe than sorry. What you don't know won't hurt you." This meant, "don't meddle, or don't butt in where you don't belong"; an effective way to enforce silence or independent investigation. Unfortunately, the admonitions may have unintended results. There is a tale about a shipwrecked sailor, out on a lone rocky islet in the sea. He found a fungus that shone in the dark and, using it as ink, he scrawled a message crying for help, and sent it out on the waters, on a piece of bark. There is a quick end to this tale. The sailor died of starvation. It turned out that the fungus he was using was edible.

A "worthless woodlot," costing only twenty-five dollars an acre, might tempt you to think that the country people must have held the land in low esteem. In fact, smaller cultures, whose inherited memories of the land are not for sale, have shared much more personal and rooted feelings for it than mass cultures that simply leave before they move in. The pressures of overcrowding and mechanical reactions to things tend to detach us from a land and from our neighbors. Commodity and money-driven as we are, we can put any price on the land that the traffic will bear and be indifferent to it at the same time. But the land is not an extinct species, or we would follow in its train. All earth rises with it in the dawn, and goes down to sleep in its darkness. We neglect our own interior when we ignore its needs. I come upon the new spaces of light and fire in the darkness of the ground and know where I belong.

A Shining Fish

I have never seen a more improbable looking fish than the ocean sunfish, *Molla molla*. As described in Henry B. Bigelow and William C. Schroeder's *Fishes of the Gulf of Maine* (1953), it "suggests the head and foretrunk of some enormous fish cut off short." It has a very small mouth at the top of its snout and just behind and on line with the mouth are its very small eyes. The gill openings are also remarkably short and small. A long but narrow caudal fin extends like a scalloped band around the end of its round, or oblong body. It has two stiff fins, like opposite propeller blades which it cannot lay back, as other fishes do. The sunfish though can move slowly through the water by waving its fins from side to side. It looks highly implausible when you see it out of water, and clumsy enough to excite ridicule, or be used by the shameless for target practice. Those who look for quick moving symmetry in fishes don't quite get it.

Darcy Thompson, in his book *On Growth and*

Form (1961), includes a drawing of this strange fish. The ocean sunfish is a striking example of "deformation," changes of shape within a given form. Thompson compares the sunfish with another species, the porcupine fish. On the surface, at least, they do not look very much like each other, to the untrained eye. But, Thompson shows through the use of a mathematical system of concentric circles and coordinates, that the fish can be seen to share a common form. When the two are compared, bone by bone, it is possible to reconstruct the skeleton of one from the skeleton of the other, which seems to suggest that consistency of form over evolutionary time is also subject to inner transformation, as fishes in their watery medium pulse ahead like waves in their everlasting travels across the globe. The ocean sunfish belongs in the same realm of oceanic artistry and power as all the others.

On a fine day in October, with only moderate seas, I joined a crowd of passengers on an excursion out of Provincetown, to look for whales. Only a few years ago a sportfisherman told me that the ocean waters off Cape Cod were crowded with whales, porpoises, tuna, and a myriad of seabirds. I have no idea what lay behind this impression, but the numbers do not hold up. As we moved past Race Point and headed farther out, we spotted only one small minke whale and two finbacks. We were told that the great whales including the humpbacks—always looked for because of their often spectacular leaps and plunges—have gone somewhere else. They may have migrated from their usual range along Stellwagen Bank to outer ledges along the coast of Maine.

On our way back to port, as we looked out from the deck, a sunfish came into view, quite close to the ship. One stiff fin like a rudder protruded above the surface, and below it underwater was a large round disk, all white, but with a somewhat greenish cast. The *Molla molla* has no scales, but it has a thick skin, about one and one half inches, which is coated with mucus or tough slime. It is host to a great variety of parasites, inside and out, some of which, creatures of the plankton, may be luminous. Its principal food consists of ctenophores, or comb jellies, voracious and highly luminescent creatures of the sea, as well as the jellyfish known as the medusa. The reason this fish shines in the dark is not because it is bioluminescent in itself, but because it takes luminous qualities from the organisms it is in contact with. Its bioluminescence is borrowed light taken into its bodily cells. So it might have been appropriate to call it a moon fish, as it carries its reflected light in the dark sea like the moon between the clouds. It is a drifter, absorbing the brilliance of the shining ocean. This amazing animal is not without some parallel to our own feelings of reality; it grunts and groans when hauled out onto the unwelcome land.

The following account of the comb jellies is taken from that captivating book, *The Open Sea*, by Alister Hardy:

> It is the comb-jellies—Ctenophora—which give us some of the most spectacular displays of brilliant flashing light in our waters. They are nearly all capable of emitting sudden vivid flashes. The sea is often full of very small young specimens, each of which may give off quite a bright flash. They are excellent animals to use for demonstrations of spontaneous luminescence. A plankton sample containing these animals can nearly always be relied upon to give a good show—but we must remember that they do not perform at all until they have been in the dark for almost twenty minutes. If you intend to show your friends a good display you must keep your sample of plankton completely covered with light-proof cloth, or in a light-proof cupboard, for this length of time before bringing it out for exhibition in the darkened room.
>
> As a young student I once had an amusing demonstration of this inhibitory effect of light. I had gone over to Brightlingsea to hunt at low tide

in the thick Essex mud for the rare and curious worm-like animal priapulid. It was nearly dark before I had found any and it was too late to return to Oxford that night, so I put up at a very old inn where I slept in a four-poster bed in an oak-panelled room. After a strenuous day digging in the mud I retired early and soon dropped to sleep after blowing out my candle. Later in the night I was awakened by some reveller coming noisily to bed in the room next door. I opened my eyes and blinked them with astonishment, for a number of little blue lights were bobbing about in the darkness just over the end of my bed. It was as if there were a lot of little goblins dancing up and down in the air. Before coming to bed I had of course celebrated the finding of priapulid—but only with a pint of bitter; clearly there must be some more objective explanation! I struck a match and lit the candle. I now saw that, level with the end of my bed, was the top of the chimney-piece on which I had placed a row of large glass jars filled with sea-water, with a little mud at the bottom of each containing my precious animals. Getting up and switching on the electric light I examined them closely and then saw that the water was full of very young ctenophores—*Pleurobrachia,* I think—actively swimming up and down. They had certainly not been flashing when I first turned out the light and got into bed; nor were there any flashes when I settled into bed for the second time—or rather not at once. I was now well awake, and it was some time before I could get off to sleep again; before I did so, after about twenty minutes in the dark, the little "blue devils" began their dance again.[1]

The great world ocean is a vast container of light, carried in the bodies of a multitude of living forms, born of its dark and shining depths. What can the final explanation of bioluminescence be, as it is found on land as well as in the sea? It probably begs the question from the point of view of a practicing scientist, but it might be that the supreme qualities of a medium universally shared are not subject to final solutions or analysis.

1. Alister Hardy, *The Open Sea* (Boston: Houghton Mifflin, 1956).

Metamorphic Time

If I wake up early enough to see it on a clear day, a great band of color crosses the horizon above the line of trees, at times on a rising wind, and I am lifted into a communion with life's inescapable ancestry. There is no way out of it. I see with every other form of life that is capable of seeing. I am not on Standard, Daylight, or any other form of manipulated time. I exist on universal Sun Time, as its cosmic light moves into the waiting trees.

When we moved to Cape Cod some fifty years ago, we knew comparatively little about the specific nature of our surroundings. We followed others who had been attracted to a land with sheltered hollows, sea beaches, and salt marshes in a close alliance with the open waters of the Atlantic. Over the centuries, the settlers had cut down much of the wooded growth that covered the Cape's inland miles, but the pitch pines and oaks that tolerate sandy, dry soils have grown back, along with many introduced species that were never native to the place. The Cape had a long period of slow growth and accommodation, in spite of the changes brought to it by the white settlers, the small farmers, and the shore fishermen, some of whose names are still in evidence, but it is no longer blessed with at least semi-isolation. The twentieth century has not been inclined to leave it that way.

When we moved in, the town of Brewster had only nine hundred inhabitants; its population has now risen to nine thousand. Much quicker and easier access was made possible by the construction of the Cape Cod Highway, plus the straightening and "improvement" of local roads. We have not yet learned that the straight line, and linear time, can never improve on a land held together by elastic ways of reaching its own destinations. A new and crowded impermanence invades the land. Hundreds of thousands of people come and go without a sense of reliance on the local weather and the tides. Fortunately the clouds float free of us, and the waves keep rolling in along the shore, and the alewives, or freshwater herring, still migrate inland in the spring, to rediscover those unfailing passages in their memories, which never had time or direction imposed upon them.

The box turtle has calmly and slowly moved through these woods for a thousand years. Its eggs are laid in sandy cuts and clearings, at times bordering old roads. Skunks would come routinely and dig them out, a handy source of food; but what reduced these older inhabitants to a pitiful few was the increase in automobiles and trucks, which frequently ran them over. Another widespread threat to their local existence came from the summer tourists who took them away as pets to some city apartment. In this way, a location and its embodiment are lost.

The real natives, who can also tell us where we are, must include the mushrooms, which I started to look at more closely as a result of the woodpile. Some grow, change shape, and then disappear at what appear to be arbitrary times, as if they were responding to some subterranean influence, playing games with our expectations.

Throughout a violent century that has almost introduced homelessness as a way of life, I have found myself trying to catch up with a more rooted past which I had lost and left behind me. I was in dire need of a consistency I could rely on. It took me a long time, many years of concentration on the details of an almost forgotten nature, to find that it had never really left me. I had to meet the water, the soil, and the ever patient trees again to find out, as John Muir did, heading for the sunset over the waters, that going out is really going in.

I still have no idea whether or not science has a definitive explanation for the phenomenon of bioluminescence, in a mushroom, rotting wood, dead fish, plankton, or fireflies. After many years in the pursuit of natural history, I am always meeting deeper waters that elude my own awareness. What lies behind the names that are so readily available to us, but the unexplored distances followed by other forms of life?

The fox fire in the woodpile was not only a revelation of what we had never noticed before. The slow process of decay and regeneration was going on, not only a hundred yards from our house, but all around us. We had only walked by, as if that fire of association could never touch us. Obviously, living on top of the world is no proof of success.

How can we know the real worlds of life without being engaged in their ritual and ceremonial behavior? Their beauty is born of the elements and the great spaces they occupy. So, the blue damselflies speed back and forth across the surface of an inland pond like splinters of glass, brilliantly partaking of the nature of light on all the waters.

The two seasons of autumn and spring, on the two ends of winter, share at least one similarity. They are periods of travel and relocation, on a major scale. The Cape, like a bended arm thrust out from the mainland, is in the path of innumerable migrants of the air and sea. I find in my notes that back in the 1960s a sandhill crane was reported to have landed at First Encounter Beach in Eastham, perhaps part of a migratory flock headed toward wintering areas along more southerly shores. They fly at great heights, often too high for ground observers to see, and have a trumpeting call. In early November a few years ago, I received a letter from the Great Plains which brought exciting news: "The Sand Cranes are in the sky today, with a great announcement and celebration of distance and time."

I watch flocks of birds flying through the silvery light of evening, and I am aware that they are bound out, not carrying mechanical aids and substitutes for location, but relying on ancestral ways irrepressibly uniting space and inner timing. For the most part, in a temperate zone, we think of the four seasons as quite distinct from each other, associating the autumn with leaf color and the winter with snow, but all years flow into each other, and one season is a transformation of another. The earth is being continually transformed into changing states of being, and we will never have a true understanding of where we live without engaging our feelings with it.

Each day and night moves by carrying countless variations and variables on a theme of consistent change. As we are moved into shorter hours of daylight and colder nights, there is nothing in the sentient land that does not move with the great following waves of planetary motion. The slow-growing lichens on the rocks and trees that cover our hillside at all times of the year seem to carry a special affinity in the fall for the weather that invades us. They are of a gray-green color that retains a cooler light and a condition of moisture that reflects their proximity to the ocean from which the cool gray fogs drift in. It is not "adaptation" or "seasonal adjustment" alone that can explain the new season of light. What we passersby must see as a repetitious series of often wasted days leaves no room for the hidden fires of nature, which occasionally bring reality, like that wasp which just stung me in the back of my neck.

An urbanized world that requires everyone to use artificial light as a substitute for what comes to us through the sun and the stars will not soon escape the truth that comes from below. Put us in a deep cave without a shred of light and we are still aware of the periods of daylight and dark-

ness. We are born inheritors of states and conditions we share with the land itself, and its retain-
ers. One day, perhaps, enough people to make a
difference might get together and come to the
conclusion that we are on the same level as the
insects, which might serve not to lower but to
heighten our sense of self-esteem.

The passage of the season as it is followed by
the other than human lives around us cannot be
measured by our own time-keepers, or by an in-
sanely divergent economy; this passage is the
prerogative of the light, intercepted by a falling
leaf or the scales of a fish. Mercurial light flashes
on the surface of a rock that 'over millions of
years, will be reduced to sand on a glittering
beach, and it can be seen in a quicksilver shower
of rain. The transformations carried through all
seasons are more magical than fact, but to follow
them is to sense where safety lies. In quick per-
ception lies the hunger of reality. We can never
fully understand where we are without letting in
the interceptors of light, on terms of equality. We
can rise no higher.

One late autumn day in New Hampshire
when long shadows covered the lower slopes of a
small mountain, and the coming night promised
frost on the pumpkin, I looked into the interior
of a big moss-covered log, what was left of an old
sugar maple. There I saw a mourning cloak but-

terfly, as it was lightly crawling in to what might be a long winter's sleep. The mourning cloak, first to appear in the spring, is also one of the few butterflies that hibernate. Hibernation as described in the dictionary is a state of torpor brought on by increasing cold. To take the term out of context, hibernation may also be allied, I suppose, to various states of semi-hibernation, the suspension of the faculties, as well as what we experience as half-sleeping, and dreaming states of mind.

If we do not crawl into a log and go to sleep, or hole up for months inside an ice cave like a polar bear, against the implacable arctic night, we avoid extremes, and have conscious ways to protect ourselves from them. We are a singularly frail species when caught out in the open. Our dreams, which some people suppress, or fail to understand, follow us into the daylight. The unconscious like a dark underground river carries us on into the unknown, and death, which the poet Yeats said man invented, is indistinguishable from life in all its journeys.

Butterflies spread their wings for the flowers they feed on in the sequential order of their appearance. The span of life for most butterflies is short, as it fits the rhythms of the season they were born to. We wait for them to appear, sipping nectar from the blossoms, and then forget them. They are or seem to be, as ephemeral as the flowers themselves, but their special artistry springs of a permanence in the underlying orders of life which we can only try to follow.

Here we are, counting time as usual, in our pursuit of it, with predatory feelings and a fear of failure in our heads, while the earth's wings fly by, unseen, moving on like messengers from another world. In early spring, the butterflies emerge out of various stages of resurrection, from the dark ground, the bark of trees, and fly into the nameless light and air.

It has always seemed to me that mimicry and color affinity in insects, animals, fish, and amphibians, across vastly dispersed regions of the earth must be a greatly undervalued subject. The idea that what we are looking at in a tree frog that changes its own color to fit the environment it lands in only amounts to camouflage is to neglect a highly complex form of spontaneous expression. A neighbor of ours in Maine lives in a house which has an open porch, or deck, that is bordered on one end by a tree whose leaves and branches extend into it. A gray tree frog lived there in the summertime. While it was in the tree it turned as green as a leaf. Periodically, it would leap down onto the sunny surface of the deck railing, and its color changed to the gray of the wood. It would also move onto some asphalt siding on the house where it turned black, and invisible. Their black and white cat, a mighty hunter, was completely confused by these maneuvers. She kept looking for the frog where she had just seen it, but it was no longer there, or so she thought. It had turned into a grey patch of weathered wood, only yards away from those keen eyes, which goes to show, I suppose, that our lines of sight may be perpendicular to each other but fail to meet. (For those who are addicted to clean golf courses and perfect lawns, no weeds tolerated, the grass is green because we put it there).

The wings of the mourning cloak are of a rich, dark brown, iridescent when looked at closely. They have blue dots along their inner edge, and a wide border of creamy yellow suggesting a cloak. Their color is like the wood of trees. They range widely over the woodlands and forest openings of North America. Soon after a few mourning cloaks had begun to appear, I watched one as it flew up in front of me from the driveway and open, sunny glade that faces our woodpile. It was flying low over the ground, circling back and forth, over the patterns of shadow and sunlight made by the overhanging trees, as if engaged in a participatory dance. That butterfly was a principal actor on a far wider stage of sentient life and history than we can recognize at first glance.

In the following passage from Edwin Way Teale's book *Autumn Across America,* the mourning cloak shows some unexpected behavior. They are not true migrants like the famous monarch, with its long, overland flight to Mexico; they are emigrants, occasionally moving out when their habitats are seriously disrupted, or because of a population explosion. They seem, in any case, to take some part in the wide dispersal, and often irregular behavior, that turn this great season into one of relocation on a major scale.

Red admirals, small brown skippers, sulphurs, even white cabbage butterflies pressed forward over the sand and out across the water. Each determined insect was beating its wings rapidly, forging slowly ahead into the wind. None we saw returned. Several wasps, some *Polistes,* followed the spit to its end and then headed away over the lake along the same path the monarchs were taking. Both the spicebush swallowtail and the giant swallowtail have been reported leaving Point Pelee along this same migration trail. The most surprising butterfly I saw that day heading south toward the far-off Ohio shore was the mourning cloak. This species hibernates in hollow trees and under debris to appear—"the thaw butterfly"— during the milder days of winter. Yet here it was, starting like a monarch across the thirty-five miles of open water in a definite southward movement.

I have come to believe that these butterflies may move about in fall more than is realized. On a more recent September day, I drove the fifteen miles between Jones Beach and Captree along the ocean front on the south shore of Long Island. In that fifteen miles I encountered twenty-five mourning cloaks. They were all flying in the same direction, southwest, along the same path being taken by the migrating monarchs. All were heading in a straight line, all were flying steadily, all were maintaining a speed of about fifteen miles an hour. It may be that such autumn movements of mourning cloaks are a kind of partial migration, a pilgrimage to more favorable hibernating areas.[1]

In the fall of the year, together with all the other signs of outer and inner migration, the famous monarch butterflies gather, and can be seen flying down the mountain slopes and hillsides, over spent cornfields, meadows, and fields, as well as high overhead, moving south. No other butterfly makes an annual migration, as the birds do, from north to south, out of one hemisphere to another. Our eastern variety flies all the way to Mexico, where it winters in the

1. Edwin Way Teale, *Autumn Across America* (New York: Houghton Mifflin, 1950).

high-altitude forests of the Sierra Madre mountains. On the other hand, as Robert Michael Pyle's *Field Guide to the Butterflies* (1991) will tell you, no single individual makes the entire round-trip journey. Although they have large wings, it must seem to anyone like a prodigious journey for a creature no bigger than a leaf.

The pigment on the scales of their fiery, red orange wings takes its color from the sun's spectrum, and the black lines on the veins of their wings suggest the night on the sun's far side. When I, with a number of other enthusiastic volunteers, were starting in on a teaching program for the newly formed Cape Cod Museum of Natural History, I began to be aware of some of the hidden dimensions behind the common sights and events that I had only taken for granted. We had kept and cultivated a small patch of milkweed on the land we had purchased for the museum, and there I was able to witness the four stages through which the monarch, one of the "milkweed butterflies" comes into being.

The green of the milkweed host follows the process from minute green eggs, to the shining green of the marvelous chrysalis. The handsome caterpillars are white, with black and yellow stripes. The chrysalis is the final state in a slow, gradual, and meticulous two-week process, one that might be said to follow death and resurrection the whole way. As Jo Brewer describes it in her book *Wings in the Meadow,* each step in the process of change from one form to another seems poised at the brink of finality.

> In one moment, Danaus would either live or die
> . . . for the larva it was a ceremony marking the acceptance of death at the end of life, tempted by centuries of intuitive knowledge that life, in turn would follow this seeming death. For, whether he knew it or not, the larva was already dying. He had been dying since his wandering began. He could no longer eat, and his powers of regeneration and ambulation were gone.[2]

When I saw the monarch chrysalis for the first time, a jade green pendant jewel with a gold circlet around it, I was unable to take it in. The pure gold color was difficult to understand, as if all gold must be authorized by the human race. Then it began to change to blue, almost translucent, with the dark shadows of the folded wings beginning to appear, before the monarch was born, starting to unfold and flex its muscles in the sunlight.

Obviously, what I had been introduced to was never the result of human invention, some manufactured product on its way to rule or ruin. Our conscious world might see in terms of the long

2. Jo Brewer, *Wings in the Meadow* (Boston: Houghton Mifflin, 1967).

process of evolution, but for a temporary on-looker like myself, this planetary art, the perfect, lasting form, seemed to recognize no point of departure, to be out of distances unseen by the human mind. We lay waste the earth, destroying it with substitutes, desperate to succeed, but the real images of perpetuity come to life again, under the pendulum of the sun.

The Source of the Brook

Our modern success in changing the face of the earth over once immeasurable distances has not yet destroyed the prodigious patience of the trees. When I go back to my boyhood home in New Hampshire, I meet them again, spreading new branches across the path in front of me, as if to remind me that I once swung on them in passing, when they and I were young. Their time-holding relieves me of my own precarious hold on the years ahead.

Hiking, some years back, down from the summit of Mt. Moosilauke, north of Lake Sunapee, where I grew up, I saw that the mountainside was covered by a wide swathe of dead balsams—the result of winter storms with exceptionally cold winds that drove rime ice into their needles and tissues. Ice crystals driven by such a wind against an exposed mountainside can be lethal to its trees. This involves a much more dynamic process than what is often called a blowdown. Foresters refer to it as "fir waves." These waves progress in the direction of the prevailing wind, the end of a wave coming when it passes over a ridge. Yet even here, recovering is in the nature of a tree. A young hemlock may stand in the dense shade of mature trees with a potential life span of four hundred years, or more. And so it may stay the same height for nearly half a century. When some overshadowing giant crashes at last, letting in the sun, the young tree starts to grow into the opening and gain in height.

What can life hold for us that equals the suspension of growth and time in a young tree? Every year, when I start our vegetable garden again, I feel that as long as I am able to dig, plant, and hoe with a will, I am resurrecting myself in the company of the soil and all its organisms. There is a delayed youth in every part of the land that is ready to be released.

The northern trees, rooted in adversity, have climbed back in to reclaim much of their rightful territory. On the other side of the road from our farm that was still in working order when I was a boy, there was a sloping hillside of close-cropped ground where goats were pastured. Today, many years after the farm and all its livestock were sold, the goat pasture has been covered by a small forest that must look to any passerby as if it had always been there. I suspect that the trees have a long-range memory of where they once grew and planted their own seed. The trees knew New Hampshire for thousands of years before we named it; it belongs to them in the fullness of time, and not their replacements. The forests grow in again to shade the springs that only dry up when we abandon them.

One day when my father and I were walking down a woodland path that led from our house to the shores of the lake, we passed a spring whose cold, ever fresh water seeped out of the hillside behind it. Every year, I used to clear out the leaves that filled it and I hung a cup there on a stick for the thirsty. "That," said my father, "is the best water in the state."

Nothing is so confusing in our minds, so degrading in its effects, as the claim of a bloated industrial society to preeminence over the face of the earth. The great forests, the lungs of the planet, are ravaged and idly destroyed. The waters of the earth are polluted, and we do not recognize the difference when we drink of the real thing. We tend to think of the abiders in nature as inessential or strange. The integrity of any land slips away in proportion to our indifference. I count on the presence of that inconspicuous spring to help me recognize an imperishable truth, born of a greater land that has not yet forced me into exile.

Past the spring, down a narrow fringe of sandy beach bordering the shore, is the outlet of the brook that used to provide water for our house, built by my grandparents late in the nineteenth century. The demands of the house, lawn, and garden increased over the years, but the volume of water pulled from the brook was not seriously reduced until the hurricane of the 1938. This famous and unexpected storm broke down and uprooted vast numbers of trees in the watershed, with the result that we had to start to pump in household and drinking water from the lake, whose essential cleanliness and purity was seldom questioned in those days.

The brook that had served the practical needs of our family for many years was on the fringe of cultivation. We passed over it many times where a bridge covered the road leading to the farm, but in many respects it was unexplored territory, steeped in its own light and darkness, like a wonderful grove of tall, white pines that lined the road.

As children, my sister Adele and I played on the small beach near the outlet of the brook, but seldom explored it. Perhaps we were held back by parental warnings. But I sensed a dark magic there, and unknown spirits in the woodlands beyond it. Huge, moss-covered boulders, dark pools where water insects twitched and skated over a surface half-lit by filtered sunlight, shallow streambeds with stepping-stones for a crossing, unnamed birds in overhanging branches, turned it into an unfinished stage. The players retreated beyond my vision. I had no notion of where those waters originated. Perhaps I was not encouraged to ask. Anything had beginnings. Nothing had endings, except a school vacation. For all I knew, the source of the brook was in some distant mountain I might never climb.

At its mouth, the brook flows out over a shallow, sandy bottom into the lake. This is where rainbow smelt come in to spawn upstream after the ice has melted. It is a landlocked variety of the marine smelt common to numerous streams and rivers along the coast. Several years ago, I saw many of their silvery, semitransparent bodies lying on the sand, half-mangled or chopped up. At first it occurred to me that the mutilation might be the work of landlocked salmon, fished out of Lake Sunapee for generations. As a boy, I had seen two men in a rowboat quietly fishing for them, summer after summer, in suspended animation, before the lake got too crowded and noisy with motorboats. But the salmon do not mangle their meals. They will feed on schools of smelt as they rise toward the surface. It was evidently a playful and well-fed otter, recently seen farther up the brook, and not the salmon, who was responsible.

Farther up the brook, I have sometimes caught sight of fingerling brook trout, colorful, but very wary, as they flashed out of sight, on feeling the reverberations of my footsteps on the bank. The water striders on the surface of the pool make dark dimpled shadows, reflected on the stones beneath them. The deer move in and out of the wood on their slender legs to drink, and coons dig crayfish out of the shallow edges of the brook. The dark and glossy coated mink moves stealthily up and down the watercourse, seldom seen by passerby. In the deeper parts of the woodlands and forests is another famous furbearer, the fisher, or "fisher cat," as I have heard it called by the natives. It hunts red squirrels from branch to branch across the trees with a fierce and restless rapidity. It is also the only predator of porcupines. It will bite their nose and flip them on their backs, to eat the undersides. But the only one I ever saw was a dead one on the road, hit by a car, and another, a young female in temporary captivity, in a cage.

Wherever he goes, treating nature as his surrogate, modern man wants his questions answered. "What is it worth?" "What does it do?" If satisfied, he does not linger in the recesses and shadows of life's forests, but moves on, out of reach, deserting thousands of years of interactive life. The secret, sensory languages of a forest elude us, as if we were out of practice in conversing with our own ancestry.

As the deer move out over open ground, their awareness is acute. Not the slightest sound or chance motion escapes them. They know when we come in; they know where we have been after we leave. The space in a forest is like a room where we are unable to see out to the other side. For a long time, however, deer hunters have set up deer stands, plank seats high in the trees where they could wait for the animals as they moved into range. They take advantage of the fact that deer, in spite of their great eyes, are unable to see high over their heads.

The brook descends the westward facing slopes of Sunset Hill, so named by my grandparents, who used to ride or walk up to the summit, a brow of sloping granite, surrounded by a fringe of low trees. Dark green mountains rolled out westward with the fires of the sun; and the shores of the sparkling lake far below them were all that showed any signs of habitation. Who could resist the promise of such a world?

The watershed of the brook comprises some 320 acres of a 675-acre tract given by my father,

Clarence Leonard Hay, to the Society for the Protection of New Hampshire Forests in 1960. The brook is their central artery. Much of this land was logged, or cut over for fields and pastures by hillside farmers, and is now composed of second- or third-growth trees. The original forest may have been dominated by red spruce, but after the farms were abandoned, other trees, white pines, hemlock, maples, and birch, came back with a will to claim their space.

Throughout several centuries of settlement, with small farms and minor roads, the landscape was never so changed that it could not grow back in a relatively short period of time. The underlying character of a land held in the grips of rock, water, and the roots of trees is not easily eliminated. The traveling clouds, which we can never cut down, are also true to the nature of what lies below them. Even the wind moves according to the time-honored direction of the trees.

One fine day in early autumn, when the leaves of the swamp and sugar maples began to show tints of pink and red, David Anderson and I set out to climb up Sunset Hill and follow the brook to its source. Dave now leads the Forest Society's Land Study Center at the John Hay National Wildlife Refuge, which was named for my grandfather, poet and statesman, who served as secretary of state during the administration of

Theodore Roosevelt, the great originator of conservation law and the national park system.

We started up at the point where the "old county road" once led to the village at the south end of the lake; its wagon tracks are still visible. In the early 1960s, the Soil Conservation Service had built a small pond nearby, with water diverted from the brook, for use in case of a forest fire. A family of beaver moved in after that, and built a dam and a lodge on the downstream side. Four more dams followed, down the course of the brook, as the beaver used up the trees along the way. Their last effort was abandoned in 1994. When I last saw this dam, it seemed massive to me. It was about four feet high and thirty feet long, but the beaver had moved on, having used up their food supply. They had left a long, wide swathe of wet meadow behind them, where a few isolated trees stood out like skeletons. The beaver people, like human lake dwellers of long ago, who left traces of the pilings that held their dwelling above the water, never left a wasted and impoverished land behind them. The ancient waterways of a continent are in the minds of the beaver. They have a deep sense of the nature of water and how it moves. They could never destroy the very source of their well-being and their future; and some day, they will return. They leave new growth behind them when they press on. The wide opening made by the meadow has been of great benefit to other woodland dwellers, such as the mink, the otter and the wild turkey, deer and moose, as well as the black bear that move in to feed on the wild berries starting to flourish on the edges. Many species of birds have also been attracted to the beaver wetland; and it is a new source of nurture and protection for frogs and salamanders.

Along the old road above the meadow, tiny yellow gold frogs, the young of the year, jumped out of the grass. The spring peepers, or *Hyla crucifer,* so called because of the smudged black cross on their backs, and the wood frogs were the most visible. The peepers begin to sing in all healthy wetlands as the winter retreats, with a primal intensity that little else can equal. The frogs and salamanders in their courtship rituals and seasonal transformations have mysterious alliances with the medium of water itself, in its changing nature. We walk over a great underworld of knowing and sensuous relationships. On the surface, we may know the details of the shape-changing universe of frogs or butterflies, but fail to give it much connection with ourselves. Familiar, goggle-eyed frogs, once a favorite subject of country humor, are beginning to disappear, in many parts of the world. They are casualties of the poisons that we easily and idly let fall over the entire face of the earth, even when we are unable to predict the consequences of what we do. We have all become invisible destroyers who are incapable of identifying our victims. This can only be highly disturbing and frightening to those who are aware that their own, personal ties to the land are being frayed to the limit. It is as if we looked down into the surface of any stream and failed to find our own reflection there.

Dave and I trudged slowly uphill, following the course of the brook. We caught sight of a hole in the bank, occupant unknown, and passed under a tree where some raptor, probably a hawk had perched for a while, judging by the white droppings on the ground. Then we came on the raised mound of what was once the root mass of a big tree, probably a vestige of the '38 hurricane, and saw a red eft lying there, as brilliantly colored as a devil dancer in some medieval painting, clearly outlined on the reddish brown form of the once living tree. It looked as supremely confident as a skunk, which knows that it is normally free from attack. The red eft is the juvenile phase of the eastern newt, which inhabits lakes, ponds, and slow-moving streams. It has a poisonous toxin in its skin. This enables the newt to swim at a depth of thirty feet in a lake without being devoured by fish. The eft wanders through moist woodlands for as long as seven years before returning to water to be transformed into an adult, aquatic salamander.

The charmed life once attributed to salamanders in less scientifically minded days probably owes as much to the nature of water as to fire, both partners in magic. Mercurial, chimerical water, flowing across the land and seeping through the soil, is the living agent of all transformations.

The tan, leaf-colored wood frog, with its black face mask, reverses the breeding cycle of the newts. Their eggs are laid in early spring in ponds or temporary vernal pools that may still be partially covered with ice. As they develop, the young move out onto the woodland floor. A wood frog, with its highly distinctive color and design, honors the environment of which it is a part. I remember picking one up out of another forest floor many years ago. As I held that perfect creature in my hand, so close to me, and still so far removed, I gave up all pretensions.

Farther uphill, the woods were increasingly full of the signs of travel. We met the great stout body of a yellow birch, probably 200 to 240 years old; it was hollowed out at the base of the trunk, a cavity full of wood shavings and dung. This was the home of a porcupine. In one of Richard K. Nelson's books about the Koyukon Indians, he quotes one of them as saying: "The porcupine knows Alaska like you know the palm of your hand."

We walked past a line of young swamp maples, whose bark was stripped off by the lower incisors of a moose. The tracks of moose and deer appeared on the trail, their hoof prints clearly outlined in the dark mud, like some prehistoric markings on a rock. Because the brook's watershed is under conservation, it serves as a corridor for such travelers from the hills beyond it, a link between distance and space.

The banks along the brook grew steeper. As I looked across it, I could see the understory of trees on the far side, so loaded with a rich flood of sunlight that they looked as if they carried its weight on their leaves.

We had seen bear scat near the trail, and had looked for claw marks on a tree, which were reported to be numerous on the far side of Sunset Hill, where there is a grove of beech trees. During the autumn months, beechnuts are one of their favorite foods. One bear had been seen sitting in a big beech, breaking and bending down the branches so as to make a feeding platform, where it could eat nuts at its leisure. They are part of a domestic economy that we, busy in our narrow kitchen, are not aware of.

A solitary vireo was flying back and forth over the brook, working it for insects, that irrepressible tribe so essential to all life in a forest. Many more birds were traveling through the leaf canopy ahead of us, part of assemblies that precede outward migration. They included chickadees, as well as juncos or "snowbirds," so familiar to New Englanders during the winter months. Various species of warblers flitted through the leaves. Among these were yellow-rumped warblers, black-throated greens, blackburnians chestnut sided. The naturalist Edwin Way Teale called them "rainbow birds." With their sun-inspired colors, they carry the spirit of the rain forests north each year to blend with the northern trees. Then we came on what we had set out to find. Under the brow of a steep slope not far from the summit, where the brook and its moss-covered rocks went no farther, was a wide, light green circle on the ground, covered with water-loving plants. The ever-flowing waters seeped out of this spring to be carried down, century after century, trickling through a far-reaching network of roots and associated fungi, feeling their way through the soil to a great wilderness lake. The brook has guarded all the secrets of the forest, as well as its own origins, which lie at an unknown depth in the bedrock of this minor mountain. I once unconsciously drank of its waters, and for much of my life I had been far removed from it, but now I had come home, to the center, the waiting heart, which was not ours to claim alone.

We can easily turn ourselves into outsiders, blinded by the tormented world we have made for ourselves, but we are incapable of replacing the truth. I once peered in at an early age and sensed the magic in that brook, but I was never fully aware of how much promise it carried with it. This time, I remembered my father, a sensitive and generous man, who knew that we can never tell the land what it is meant to contain; you have to wait for it to tell you.

A stand of hemlocks, lover of steep slopes and ravines, grew across from the charmed circle of the spring. During the coming winter, it would provide shelter, and a stronghold, for deer and moose. As Dave and I started to walk back downhill, we looked down at the brook and its deep pools and spoke of trout that would soon lie there in a state of torpor, concealed by a cover of ice, waiting to be freed by the everlasting springtime.

A local land speculator bought up the large tract of land that includes the top of a high hill adjacent to Sunset Hill. The entire top of it had been shaved of its trees, and was now covered with wide access roads, all previous tracks and trails banished to the hinterland. This "blasted heath," to quote from the tragedy of *King Lear,* was now with unconscious irony, called "High Meadow." The few trees left standing on the site intended for development were completely isolated from each other, and would not last long. They were pitilessly exposed to those icy gales which feel as if they had come straight from the North Pole. The natives call it the "Montreal Express." The view out from the bare slopes was nothing less than a panorama at its most extravagant. Whole worlds had been blown open for the human eye. Way down, lying below the steep hillside, was the eleven-mile-long lake, with a rare mineral shine. To the north the great range of the White Mountains was now in plain view.

The last time I saw this development, the dimensions of one of the houses in the process of construction were six thousand square feet. The new owners, who came from out of state, were summer residents, and would never have to tackle the winter head on. If obliged to, they would be protected and fully compensated for any hardships that might result.

Later in the season, after many leaves had fallen, and the sky started changing from gold to gray, while the wind tossed in a few pockets of snow, a moose ran through "High Meadow." He was in full rut, and his tongue was hanging out. He turned away and ran out, realizing perhaps, that he was intruding on a new world of property rights. A beat-up black pickup truck with Vermont plates had driven in and its owner was talking to a carpenter who would remain all winter working on the house. The truck bore a bumper sticker that read: "Eat the rich."

The Sea in the Land

On a brief trip to Cape Cod, back in September of 1853, Ralph Waldo Emerson wrote in his journal of visiting Nauset Light on the back side of the Cape, where he talked with the lighthouse keeper: "Collins, the keeper told us he found obstinate resistance on Cape Cod to the project of building a lighthouse on this coast, as it would injure the wrecking business."

Looting ships wrecked along the shoreline was a highly profitable nineteenth-century business. The wreckers, who were plentiful, did not fancy lighthouses that might prevent prize wrecks which could furnish whole houses.

Emerson's journal account echoed what many observers have said about the Cape. It had an "emaciated appearance," he wrote, like the Orkney Islands off the north of England: ". . . the starkness of the country could not be exaggerated." The wind, he said, "makes the roads . . . and a large part of the real estate was freely moving back and forth in the air." Collins, the keeper, told Emerson that he had been to Indiana, where he felt stifled by all the hills, and ". . . longed for the Cape, where he could see out."

Like my worthless woodlot, real estate on the Cape, another wrecking business, still rests on sand. Cape Cod, after all, is a product of glaciation and the North Atlantic and its close alliance with the sea has always attracted people to it. But the trees, primarily pitch pine and oak, with some locusts, have grown back after several centuries of cutting, and it is now harder to see out. The Cape is a landform where every shore, hollow, or small hill looks as if it had been molded by the waves. Storm waves, not people, make the land, and pull down cliffs on the outer shore each year. Eventually, the Cape will be lost under the rising sea.

Since the white colonists settled there, the Cape acquired a reputation for stability and the quiet life. Before the modern highways came in, it was not easily reached and the inhabitants enjoyed a reprieve from the assaults of a stampeding nation. Small-scale farmers and shore fishermen, those who used the salt marshes for salt hay for their livestock, and speared eels in the channels, built their houses and barns back from the shore. And the centuries passed them by.

Then a new kind of transience succeeded slow travel, and the daily routine of going down to the salt flats at low tide to dig for clams. The space between town centers once comfortably removed from each other started to fill with temporary and exchangeable houses with no centers at all. Indian burial grounds were buried under developments and supermarkets, and local footpaths lost their names. After World War II, fast traffic and new highways came in, in a perpetual state of "improvement." Land prices skyrocketed. The "worthless woodlot" was no more. Fast travel put everyone on wheels, now empowered to reach any corner of the land, or nowhere, whenever a person felt inclined. Space was now at a premium, and all shores were quickly reached. A habit of mind set in that was far less interested in a land once valued for subsistence living than it was in resale value or proximity to an ocean view. Millions of people live along the Atlantic seaboard with their backs to the sea, but seldom lay eyes on it, or touch it. The great ocean lies out there like a flat, geographic map, which can be seen only from the top of a high office building.

Much of the year, the cars speed by at high velocity on any road. They look as if they had been shot ahead by some mechanical sling, like those clay pigeons once used by sportsmen for target practice. The world is full of angry, restless drivers, too busy to look beyond themselves, and every morning, without exception, injury and death from automobile accidents is on the news.

Native species of plants and animals have begun to disappear. That great American forest bird the ruffed grouse is gone from the woods by our house, possibly because of domestic cats that prey on ground-nesting birds. The same is true of that loud cryer of the night, the whippoorwill, which no longer disturbs our sleep, and the beautiful chiming of the wood thrush is seldom heard. Few people notice this loss of sound and light, as if we had all become accustomed to its absence.

A recent newspaper article pointed out that of hundreds of species of plants listed by the botanist Horace Bicknell over seventy-five years ago on Martha's Vineyard, at least a quarter are missing. But the question is raised as to whether or not they are really gone. Some naturalists suspect that many of them might still be there. What we have lost may be the motivation for finding them. There are apparently few people left "who can spot an endangered sedge grass or a pigmy shrew."[1]

1. Scott Allen, "Losing a Tie to Nature" (*Boston Globe*, 7 May 1996).

One thing I do know is that indifference is the enemy of recognition. I also believe that the more detached we become from where we live the less we will know about ourselves.

We are unable to know a land which we can leave almost as soon as we arrive. True directions come from a long acquired ancestry. I have always been impelled to visit and revisit the sea, but it was not until I saw the annual run of alewives down the road from us that I began to take in its practitioners and to give them credit for a genius of their own. Before I first saw them crowding the fish ladders that led down from the ponds where they spawn, they were only fish. I then began to see a passion, an insistence in them to keep on and never stop, that I had only dimly suspected. They were running past their own mortality.

The town's alewife warden at the time was Harry Alexander, a native Cape Codder who first told me where to find the herrin' as they spawned along the shores of the ponds. He did not explain the habits of the alewives in scientific terms. He treated them as neighbors. His experience of them was part of a lifetime of living in one place, and his speech originated in settled shores thousands of miles across the sea.

In my notes about him, I find a few phrases that are many worlds removed from the standard

TV speech of today. Who speaks of a "rum cross-ing," or "a sparky old devil" anymore? I did not get up-to-date information from him as he stood by the waters of the run and the old grist mill. His information came from experience, and he talked about the fish in the same tones he might use for the family next door. "Well, as a general rule," he said, in answer to my questions, "they come in on the seventeenth to the nineteenth of March. By the first of May they really come by the thousands, but this year the temperatures are so slowed down. The onshore winds are from the northeast. They get sand in their gills, and they won't come in. [This may have been in mid-April.] Next week we should have a lot of success. But I would not guarantee it won't be cold . . . 42 to 43 degrees in the air, and the water right down to 40."

I asked him about the fry that are hatched out from the eggs laid in the ponds, the headwaters of the brook. "Well, the youngsters go back three and a half weeks after hatching. The little fellows don't have any trouble getting back unless the flow of the stream is stopped. If you can't take care of it, they can get into trouble."

Harry was highly suspicious of people who might think they knew better than he did. He may have been deficient in science, but not in homegrown experience. His house was only a short distance from Stony Brook and the run, over which he presided in a fairly loose and un-managerial way. He was a man of rough humor and often rough moods. He lived plainly, in his own place, and so far as I know, never traveled very far, but every year the great migration came close to his doorstep. The land he lived in was at one with the sea. One day I met him and his sad-faced son, Kenneth, on the streets of Hyannis, only ten miles away from his house in Brewster. "Well, John," he said, "you are way out today." This did not imply that I was wandering in my head. "Way out" simply meant far offshore and away from home. I remember him best as a neighbor who knew where he lived, without go-ing too far to find it. At a time when I knew next to nothing about alewives, he was my indispens-able guide. Since that time, I have learned a good deal more about the biology and habits of the alewives, but nothing exceeds first meetings, on home grounds.

I suppose that most of us are inclined to think of fish as passive recipients of their environment, in spite of all the passion those inland leapers like salmon and alewives show us as they climb a rocky falls. Commodity-ridden, we hold them at a distance, as a food that is neither essential to our well-being or our future. But in a power-hungry culture do we not treat water, their great medium, in much the same way? Common utility debases it in our minds, and its universality encourages us to treat it as expendable, removed from its source.

Down at the sea's edge, where the fish nose in during the spring, and where the young leave the freshwater of their birth, they become a food of the sea. I have watched the waves a thousand times over. They roll in, one after another, like musical notes across the surface of the globe, while the tides breathe in and out rising and falling as if they were part of a vast diaphragm.

The power of the sea pulls the migrant fish into itself. Nowhere is this more impressive than in the young alewives, a few inches long, as they move out through summer and fall from the waters where they were hatched out. They leave the perch, pickerel, and sunfish behind them, to subsist within the more closed seasons of the land. Because of a serious drought several years ago, pond levels were very low and the young alewives were unable to move out of the headwaters of Stony Brook to be carried down to saltwater. I watched thousands of them as they were swinging back and forth behind an outlet in the headwaters that had been dammed up by debris. They looked like dark slivers from above, but many, in their desperate need to respond to the outward flow which was in them, had flipped out of the water and their white bellies showed against the dammed up outlet. They were not released until a few days of heavy rain raised the water level. Then they started to move out, spilling down in great numbers, day after day.

From the Cape to Canada, the adult fish remember the "home streams" where they were hatched out and started to grow. Local stocks, spending the winter miles offshore, migrate in when freshwater temperatures, which they can detect, begin to rise in the springtime. Unlike other marine fish that spend all their lives in saltwater, they move toward a complex, merging, and interchanging system of water from salt, to brackish, to fresh. And each stream differs from the other for hundreds of miles down an irregular coastline. There is more to be admired in these fish than automatic behavior. Innate reactions do not bury skill. They are as competent in their navigation as any ancient Polynesians setting out on trackless seas. These are sinuous, sensitive animals, acutely aware of their surroundings and of their place with respect to others in any given school, and they can adapt to changing circumstances. I often think that we, as thinking animals, are more automatic in our responses than we would like to believe.

Carl Breivogel of Falmouth told me that he had once been on a predawn watch for the fish as they entered a small river mouth on the south side of the Cape off Nantucket Sound. This stream had a sandy, sloping bottom, as opposed to the wider tidal inlet where Stony Brook flows out of the salt marsh off Cape Cod Bay.

He could see a big school of them, massing in the stream, heading inland. But as the dawn ushered in that universal light which floods over all the land and sea, this great assembly started to reverse course, streaming out toward the salt-waters they had come from. It was an inspiring sight. "Where," he said to the friend who was with him, "could you ever see anything more wonderful than that in all your life?"

Why did they swim away from the land? Their sensitivity to light compelled them to leave a narrow stream where they were completely exposed to the sun. There were no shadowed banks along its edges where they could hide from an ever-watchful population of hungry gulls. Not until the light began to fade late in the day would they be ready to come back out of offshore waters and head in again.

Time, as measured by the world ocean, which can flood whole continents and then recede, has no finality. The great waters suspend at the turning of every tide, and as the sea rises over thousands of years it moves gradually toward the land, casually burying mountains on the way. All containment and release is there, while outer turbulence and inner calm protect life in all its extravagant distinctions. The medium of water itself is one of great cohesion, surpassing time and all our conscious means of dissecting it, down to the millisecond. In the ocean, time is not linear, in the way we lay down our dividing lines and boundaries. If anything, it is circular, returning each day with the sun and drawing down again. We are dignified by what we can never control.

The inner passions that inspire great migrations bring past and future together across the earth. They were behind the making of cathedrals and the arts of civilization. The "dawn of art," as it has been called may go back thirty or forty thousand years, when "primitive" people drew images of great animals on the walls of caves. Did we not run with lions then? Those caves are like forgotten cathedrals, bringing the past which is in the present to light again, the reality of original creation. The bear and the aurochs are there, with the ancient horses. The salmon is carved in stone, and the image of an owl looks out at us and all the endless watchers in the night.

Pisces the fish once swam with the other constellations overhead into infinity. Now it has been replaced by the numbers game, with an illusion of power that outreaches itself, threatening everything that stands in its way. We dislocate ourselves, tumbling out of our cities to devour the plains. But when the fish return, out of the sun and the great waters, with an undeviating power in their frames, they come full circle to tell us where we are.

The Way to the Salt Marsh

From our house on Dry Hill, a name once given it by natives who knew its character, it is about two miles to the beach on Cape Cod Bay. I am now obliged to walk, except when driven, having lost my driver's license because of poor eyesight. This might be thought of as a serious handicap, if not a tragedy, by the army of drivers who fly past us every day, but walking puts me on the right level with all I have been missing in our world. I have joined up for many field trips in various parts of the world, in order to make an educated guess about what I was looking at. But behind that, deeper than any name, category, or explanation I have learned, there has always been an interior equation I have not quite reached. What lasts, in our self-made, invented society?

The oaks and the pitch pines have now grown back around us, some to a fair height, though stressed and stunted in many places by their heritage of exposure to salt-laden winds, fungus diseases, and a hundred years or more of wood-choppers. We can no longer see the water from the hill; but at some times of the year, the sea winds are almost constant. We are not so enclosed in stars and spruce as we are in Maine, but all the sky above the trees is encircled by a global light. During clear weather, the dawn over the eastern horizon is ushered in by a wide band of color changes from red and pink to saffron and gold, until the fiery, orange-red of the great eye itself lifts into the sky. As the day leaves us, the sunsets over the open shore are often spectacular, especially after a storm, and so the vast circle is round once again.

My son Charlie, his wife Joanne, and I were walking down the beach, toward the end of a wild and windy day, and at first we saw no gulls. The gulls are not only scavengers, they are long-distance watchers, scanning the shore for opportunities. They understand the tides, and move back and forth with them waiting to pick up what they leave. Further along the shore they line the banks of Stony Brook at its mouth, where the alewives move in from deep water and return.

On our walk, the wind was still very strong, and the offshore waters, rock green in color, were in a state of torment. The wind was so loud that we could hardly hear our own voices, while the waves plunged and fell for miles along the sands; but it had begun to clear and a glorious sunset was waving its flags behind the racing clouds. Suddenly a number of gulls appeared, flying low over our heads, cruising slowly into the wind, and repeatedly calling. Perhaps they were only trying to keep in contact with each other, but in that setting, their response seemed profound enough. I have seen terns fly up from their nesting colonies, as the sun was going down over the sea, and then again at sunrise, in tribute to the light. Nothing so primal passes without ceremony.

The rest of life does not lose time by exceeding the speed limit. The era of slow travel, so goes the illusion, may have been set back into oblivion, never to be restored, like the so-called "good old days." But planetary complexity is kept in order by infinite patience, and periods of time which are long enough to insure stability. So at my time of life I have a great deal of lost patience to catch up with. What can tell me anything useful about where I live except those who are still in place, like a box turtle approaching a hundred years of age without benefit of modern medicine, or a beautiful green snake once fairly common here, as slim as the grass. Grassroots insure a future in a way that the communications network ignores. All information can now be instantaneously transmitted . . . in one ear and out a million others.

As I walk down from Dry Hill, the dead, brown oak leaves, turned white by an early morning frost, are crunching under my feet. A horde of grackles with cries like rusty hinges have long since swept through these woodlands, feeding on acorns for a few days. Now a blue jay lands on a bare tree, and its pitched scream pierces the sky's vision through the branches. Why such a note of triumph, from this brassy and beautiful bird? It might be because the jay helped repopulate the continent with oak and beech trees after the last ice age, ten thousand years ago, dropping the seed as it explored new territory.

Last summer I picked up the unattached cup that held an acorn, but it was not empty. In its interior was one of those perfect and delicate constructions that preceded human ingenuity. This cup was crisscrossed by the fine threads of a spider web. At its base was a drop of water, in which a tiny larva was wiggling, and as I peered in more closely, I found a small spider lying in wait. The larva may have been one of the kind that find their way out of spent acorns. The spider was probably waiting for what small insects might fly or wander in. Spiders are highly proficient in the art of waiting. How important is a drop of rainwater or dew to their enterprise? As an amateur, I am always waiting for further insight or advice that may not be forthcoming.

During the late fall and early winter, I often hear the deep-throated hooting of a great horned owl coming out of the pitch pines. It reassures me that the landscape has not been so thinned down by our occupation as to lose one of its original inhabitants, with a voice of command.

The crows are seldom absent at any time of the year. They harass the owls. They are constantly in touch with each other. Their vocabulary seems ample for their needs, as they come together and disperse. I am sure they have a better sense of location than I do. Whenever one or more of them stop in some tree on my way, I fancy that they might be exchanging sardonic comments like: "Here comes another who does not know where he is going."

Late in the day, as darkness was coming on, toward the end of a season of migration, a troop of white-throats sped by me to land somewhere down a driveway lined by a stone wall, perhaps to spend the night. They came in with such assurance and almost military dispatch as to make me think they knew the place before they got there. Birds hold the foreknowledge of voice and place together in their memories.

I never see a white-throated sparrow without

thinking of its song, an uplifting chant out of the spiraling evergreens of the northern forest. Their high, tremulous, whistling call rises out of the sun-draped ground. It may sound like "Oh, Canada, Canada, Canada" to our ears, but this bird sings of what is, and the right place to be, and for that I dearly love it.

In all of nature there can be nothing more expressive than silence. When I think of the gentle swallows that occupy the barn loft in Maine for much of the summer, while I work below, I think of how they steady my mind. Aside from an occasional shriek of alarm as I am coming in, or leaving, they are relatively quiet. What I hear are little bursts of liquid chatter between intervals of silence. The adult birds are intensely busy flying out to catch insects and returning to their young, which gives rise to what we might call comments, or low exclamations. But as the days move on, the overall tone, like the humming in a beehive, is what tempers my mood. It is not to be deciphered on the surface. It amounts to a subterranean recognition, a compliance with the season of nature. Our barn has become a "community center" for swallows over the years, a place to which many will return. It is said that the young return to the nest where they last heard their parent's voice. That seems to imply that all life is eternally domestic, no matter how much distance is put between the traveler and the nest. As for me, I know a company of swallows, and of terns, or "sea swallows," has always added more to my interior space than I knew existed before I entered their world.

One branch of the wide band of salt marshes that extends along the shore of Cape Cod Bay is only a mile from where we live. In order to reach it, I have to cross a highway, which I regard with some suspicion. When the coast is clear, I hurry over to the other side where there is an inlet to safety. At this point there is a very small house, now an antique store, but once a liquor store where our friends and neighbors used to go to fulfill their need for spirits. It was owned by Blanch and Lloyd (pronounced "Lo-ed") Cog-geshall. Her father was a cook aboard a lightship moored off the coast.

A road near the store once crossed over the marsh to reach the small town of East Dennis, which spreads over the headlands behind the shore. This road, only a few hundred yards long, was abandoned by town authorities in the 1960s. The entrance to it has been almost closed in by thickets on both sides. Walking in over this narrow lane, I once met a cottontail which streaked across in front of me, reminding me of my own feelings when faced with a speedway.

The old road is breaking up, restored to

the status of a trail. Thick bunches of switch grass, blond and sparkling in the winter light, with their graceful, curving grass blades, are marching down the center, having thrust their way through the asphalt. These plants grow again where it was their right to grow, on the upper slopes of a salt marsh. That which is appropriate is "ecology," and is determined in the living cell.

The road was built over the marsh, and a channel was cut at one point for the tidewater to run under it. The original culvert is still there, taking the rising and receding waters from one side to the other. Late in the season, I have seen schools of alewives still racing in as they often do, trying to reach the far ends of any inland waterway. A marsh sparrow flies in low to the tall reeds that line the path and drops down to lose itself on the ground between their stalks, scurrying away like a dark mouse. In mid-January I found the intact, uneaten body of a small striped bass, possibly dropped there by a gull. That led me to think that young, medium-size bass might be wintering in the marsh ditches and channels instead of migrating offshore.

I seldom meet people on my walks during the "off seasons" before the summer crowds arrive. When I do, individuals stand out against the open expanses of the marshes in all their singularity, like a passing marsh hawk, or a great blue heron. Every word they utter, and the feelings they express, no matter what the content, seem memorable. A salt marsh sanctions space and a rooted integrity. Those who pride themselves on cramming a thousand years into a minute cannot be aware of its unending reliability.

Because of their salt-tolerant grasses, the tidal marshes are the one self-sustaining landform along the northeast coast. Millions of acres of marshland and inland wetlands have been dredged, filled, and disposed of. This has been justified on the grounds that we, and our advanced machines, can reclaim marshlands and even recreate them where there were none before. Even lakes, bays, and rivers can be turned into buildable land. So we could drain away the life blood of the continent. This staggering lack of connectedness in our minds now leads to millions tumbling out of the cities and moving on to devour the plains and the forests beyond them.

The wide, flat, and silent expanse of the open marsh lies out before us in its serenity. It is covered in wintertime with thick, coarse, brown grasses like the heavy coats of a prehistoric animal. The long sound of the surf comes in under a light fog that hides white dunes. A marsh lies in the arms of the sea.

The marsh is one of the most receptive environments on earth. It is always open to the sky and all the winds and weather that flow in and recede like the tides in endlessly recurring motion. In its own, self-generating body it accommodates innumerable forms of life all responding to that common sea. The centuries pass, and its patience deepens. Even in winter when it looks dark, brindled in color like a day that is as dark as evening, it never sleeps.

All the passing winters vary in their temper. Last year the ditches looked snow-blind, covered with ice, for many weeks. This year they have been relatively free of it. As spring begins to come on, the minnows dart in the ditches, and at the right time, the fiddler crabs emerge from their burrows. The surface waters dance like a colt frisking in a meadow. The new light is an invitation to that dance and ritual that accompanies the freedom to be. And the male redwing lifts its epaulettes in a gesture of praise. We can thank the marsh for all its transformations, and above all, for its constancy.

Life in Space

C ape Cod is in motion, and not for any of the reasons we can summon up, in our hurry to control planetary space. It moves because that is what the great sea ordained. The sea both adds to its sandy shores and takes them away, year after year, but over time it is being gradually reduced. Perhaps in another fifteen thousand years as a result of constant erosion, and a rising sea level, the Cape will be submerged, a great line of sandbars lying far offshore.

The shores on both sides of the Cape are annually worn down by storm waves. Some property owners, on the back side of the Cape facing the brunt of storms from the open Atlantic, have become alarmed enough by shifting beaches, lost sand, and undermined cottages, to call for action. They have advocated the construction of a huge seawall to barricade the shore against the power of the North Atlantic, even if it breaks the treasury.

Although we are not in synchronization with the land which so many of us no longer depend on, we are still subject to laws of motion and change which will survive us. I have walked over the salt marsh and through the town many times, and made many minor discoveries along the way, but it is the sea beyond which has always called me. I have often brought feelings of fragility with me, but I can count on its vast indifference to calm me. That which returns no immediate answers to my complaints encourages my aspirations.

Out over the sandy flats at low tide, I can see all history being carried away toward distant lands. I watch the wiggling trails of a periwinkle and think of how long it took for that small creature to get here from Europe. The empty shell of a clam brings all the voices of the sea to my ear. I have found thousands of dead shells lying out on the sands at the end of summer, for no more reason, I suspect, than the sea's almost unlimited capacity for regeneration.

"Diebacks" and overpopulation are measured by the great conditions of survival, which we are too limited to regulate. I have seen tiny, nearly invisible creatures of the plankton, twitching, and turning in cosmos of their own, behind lighted glass. The flats are pitted with endless, small holes that indicate subterranean communities that change in content and form all the way around the globe. Although our own, manufactured traffic displaces us every day, it is the calmness, the enormous holding power and containment of the earth ocean that keeps us in check, no matter how far we fly away. We cannot conquer all of space and be citizens of it at the same time.

Millions of people now exclude nature and "nonhuman" life from their daily concerns as if it could be so easily dispensed with, as if old Mother Nature has been finally brought to her knees and is no longer capable of causing us more grief. When the fragment of a meteor from Mars, two billion years old, came to light, showing possible traces of life in its chemistry, those who announced it on TV said that no amount of time and money would be spared to prove it. We would no longer be alone in the universe. It has now been revealed through the Hubble telescope that our own sun is only one of innumerable suns beyond us, stepping-stones toward the unknown. Many light-years past the Milky Way, suns and planets follow the universal light. We may not be alone or even, contrary to our hopes, unique. Yet we are always surrounded by the reception of light. How many eyes has the sea?

I think, as another winter moves out, of the flowers of late spring that cover our back meadow in Maine sloping down to tidewater. It will be covered by a broad, blazing banner of flowers, each with an "eye" at the center, facing the light. Wide swathes of yellow hawkweed are joined by Indian paintbrush. Here and there are pockets of white chickweed, like star clusters, and bunches of little bluets with an intensity of color that rivals the blue-eyed grass.

The meadow is alive with motion and receptiveness. Small brown, skipper butterflies swirl up together, and the azures, the sky-blue butterflies, fly up and pirouette like ballet dancers. (The azures I see earlier on the Cape, beginning in May, fly low over open ground nectaring on flowers of the *Arbutus,* at almost running speed. In a magical display during courtship they use their sky-reflecting wings as signals to each other.)

I sense electric affinities between the flowers and the ground from which they spring. The whole field flows with light, under cloud shadows and a gentle wind. I stand in the company of delicate powers. Natural history and ecology bring me close, but never close enough. As the season moves so does the field, from flowers to grass, from grass to snow. The flowers create their own space; they all face the light of the almighty sun, which is so close, and at the same time as incredibly distant as any other star. There is no end to this ritual.

Last year, a cold fog moved in out of a cold sea, soon after we arrived, and completely surrounded us. I walked out to the edge of the field, and there was a smell of fish. The night brings in new distinctions, as one tidal world succeeds another. When were we ever alone?

The untiring vitality that surrounds and invades us is surely not distinguished by human occupancy detached from all others. It is now acceptable to make a distinction between the non-human and the human, which effectively turns the human race into an extreme minority, and isolates the human spirit. How can we claim to be a higher order of life and dismiss all that sustains us at the same time? My admiration goes out on the tide to all forms of life that do not share my vanity.

The fog's fine screen drifts in during the early morning hours to vanish in blue air. The ceremony of the seasons passes on ahead of our short lives, changing every day. The wind and snow, fire and flood, thunder and dark rain, tell us, step by step, how it was we came to be.

Following World War II, we had dislodged whole populations from custom, place, and home, to the extent that they became almost unrecognizable. I was not sure of what I had come back to. The known world was full of closed subjects, and I began to meet No Entry signs wherever I went. The rights of possession had begun to march in. It was at this time that I read two books by Rachel Carson, *The Sea Around Us* and *The Edge of the Sea*. They had an exhilarating effect on me. How could I have missed out on the sea of life which began at our front door, and had always been waiting for me? Real space, I thought to myself, was not in human power to organize, circumscribe, and narrow down for its exclusive use; it belonged to every organism on the planet. Then the gates started to open for me, and I walked out to join the distance.

Inside the long rocky coastline of Maine are the wild gardens of the sea flourishing within the give and take of the tides that roll in from across the Atlantic. Pemaquid Point, massive shoulders of bare rock uptilted from their original beds, thrust outward to the open sea. Long, broken off and rounded forms of schist lie out like great columns from some ancient temple. People who have dared to walk out to the edge on the farthest point of the land, have been surprised and swept away by unexpected waves on a rising tide. Gray rock and shining sea seem uncompromising in their austerity. But the rock, along its cracks, pools, and fissures also protects a great variety of colorful forms of life, nourished by the clear, cold waters of the pouring tides, all the way back to the "splash zone" closest to the land.

I perch on the edge of one of the long pools behind the last outer rock wall, careful not to slip and join the surf. Stones and boulders rattle under long strands of green and yellow weed. Coralline algae clings to the rock, with tufts of Irish moss, and other reddish brown seaweed. I can see a small green crab, a northern rock crab, a red starfish, and a green anemone. Great numbers of barnacles are cemented to the rock faces, sending out feathery "feet," small nets to gather in their food, the minute organisms in saltwater. All the long rocky shoreline has a substratum made of their empty shells. When the light of the sun moves over them, all these wonderful, swarming pools share in the benefits of its light, in a graduated procession back to the limits of the land.

Lunging seas drive me from my precarious seat. I have only learned a very few of the organisms in the tide pools. Many are invisible. I have a very long way to go, even with the aid of a *Guide to the Seashore*. Thousands of secret relationships hide in these tidal arms, held in mutual balance by an incomparable artistry that eludes me. I peer in and I seem to see more than recognizable forms. These tidal pools, with often grotesque creatures from a human perspective, may be hiding places for miracles. These extravagant gardens go back to the beginnings of life. They hang on a balance with immensity. I feel that vast holding and containment in my own unexplored and waiting interiors. As the great sea rises again in its rhythmic response to the moon, I am held for a brief period of time by the magic of all I can never own.

Out beyond both rocky and sandy shores are the outriders, the seabirds that have been cruising by for time out of mind. They measure the waters of the globe, while we put them down as slaves of their food supply and victims of their environment. At the same time, we tend to victimize all environments to serve our elusive and temporary ends. In spite of a growing concern about our destructive behavior, and an increasing number of conservationists, we still treat primal life as something to subdue and conquer, as if it occupied another planet. Still the future can never be in our hands if we refuse an equation with the rest of life. We are only self-limiting, and set ourselves apart, as if the human mind needed no associates. But science is unable to prove what happened at the big bang, and the big brain has yet to prove itself.

If you want to know the sea, look for its messengers. October is the month for gannets, migrating down from their nesting sites in Canada.

On the tip of the Gaspé Peninsula, these magnificent birds nest along the high cliffs of Bona-
venture Island, in great numbers. Wary of their
formidable beaks, I once walked close enough to
them as they sat on their nests to take their pictures. They were constantly rattling and groan-
ing, and left their nests to hunt for food in the
swelling seas below them, gliding off effortlessly
with wingspread of six feet.

The northern gannet is a "plunge diver," and
may be seen off the Atlantic coast during its fall
migration. Gannets fly in wide sweeps over the
surface of the sea, hunting for schools of fish.
When they spot them, they turn, then drop on
folded wings to strike the water like a spear, leaving a visible spray behind them.

After one major storm in October, when the
wind battered the shore all night long, it began
to abate, and I walked down to the beach in the
afternoon. The waves were still plunging and
heaving for miles along the sandy shore. At one
point they had cut down the dunes and washed
tons of sand off the beach, uncovering all the
stones and boulders once buried by it.

Two young gannets, with black plumage,
forced closer to the land by the storm suddenly
swung in close to the beach, hardly a hundred
yards offshore, and then turned, to glance and

veer away, and race downwind, at great speed. These birds play a profoundly intimate role in the life of the sea, testing their powers against its own. They defeat my lazy mind.

That large sea duck, the common eider, also plays an integral part in the life of the coastal waters. The males, black and white, with a pale green wash on the back of their heads, and the females, a pine brown, migrate south from Maine and Canada, coming by the thousands during the late fall and winter to feed on mussel beds around the Cape and its islands. They are bred and born of the saltwater and the coastal islands. Whenever I see one I smell salt and weed, and feel the constant plunging and pull of the surf through rocky shores. Birds of great, stolid calm and dignity, the eiders reflect the stature of their surroundings.

There is a very large rock, just off Nauset Beach on the exposed outer shore. One day I saw a big flock of eiders on the waters nearby. They were moving slowly on the surface, perhaps waiting for a change in the tide, as the gulls do. They were facing in the direction of the rock, as the currents welled up around it. Suddenly the whole flock changed direction, streaming away from the rock, as if they were on a fulcrum of the swinging tides. Eiders ride the northern seas with an almost regal authority. They are, after all, at home in space.

Among the Pawnee, reverent watchers of the heavens, the stars were never disconnected from the Earth. Their cyclical movements were directly associated with the seasons. Part of their calendric year was divided between what they called the South Star and a small group of twinkling stars known as the Swimming Ducks. The Swimming Ducks appeared in the sky over Nebraska in February as the ice began to melt in the sloughs as the wild ducks swam out into open water. The Pawnee also observed a ceremony for the Evening Star, which appeared with the Thunder, in early spring.

Higher math may be light-years away from myth and the "primitive" observances of the changing seasons, but astronomy only reaches from where we stand.

As I mentioned before, William Butler Yeats wrote that man invented death. Man also invented the concept of time, using it in increasingly refined and meticulous ways, which led to a separation of powers between man and nature, until it was possible for a technological-industrial age to declare that Nature might only be of limited use, determined by ourselves. This might also have contributed to the idea of empty space, and the motivation to conquer it, which was our custom with unsettled land. Contrast our mathematically controlled universe with how our ancestors saw it. The constellations were rushing through space like great bulls, leaping antelopes, and deer. Eagles soared there, along with swimming ducks, and other symbols of fertility, as well as the crabs of the sea. And high in their midst was the great hunter Sagittarius, with his splendid bow and quiver of arrows that could slip through the reaches of space like silvery fishes. How we shook that enchanted universe off our backs like a dog dashing out of the water.

On a quiet day in February, the temperature was forty degrees. The waves were rippling in lightly out of a calm sea, and the flats were half-covered on a ebb tide. Suddenly, the horizon was broken by a long dark flight of shorebirds. They cruised along parallel to the beach shore, and then, with swift and simultaneous unity they landed to spread out over the sand, scurrying over the surface and pecking into it for food. It was a large flock of up to a thousand individuals, some of them gray and white sanderlings, but the majority were black and reddish brown dunlins. A dog ran out, splashing in shallow water, and they all flew up again, with an audible beating of their wings. They swung in the air like a great basket, as if thrown by a long, invisible arm. They turned with beautiful unanimity and landed again farther down the beach, to spread out, explore the beach for amphipods, or other crustaceans, which had come to the now sun-warmed surface of the sand from deeper down, where they survive in freezing weather.

These sea shorebirds are tough little "globe trotters," and would spend a few weeks more exploring the coastal sands before heading for their breeding territories in the High Arctic, all the way between James Bay, Canada, and Alaska. During the winter the dunlins feed on clams, worms, insect larvae and, amphipods, in intertidal areas down the Atlantic and Pacific coasts, as far as Mexico. Some of the Alaska birds spend the winter along the coasts of East Asia. Their breeding range from outside North America extends to Iceland, Greenland, and Scandinavia. They are also seen in Great Britain, the region of the Baltic Sea, and in far eastern Russia. There are six known species; and so, they circle the globe.

The American population of these birds dates back to the late Pleistocene. The distance of their migrations, for so small a bird, are astonishing. In flight, their cruising speed has been estimated to be between 72 and 80 kilometers an hour, and in some circumstances, such as an attack by a predatory merlin, this may exceed 150 kilometers an hour.

To watch those shorebirds fly in to a bare, relatively empty beach, whose ribbed sands extended toward an unseen horizon, was like being visited by brilliant strangers from the moon. But in their reaching, they were an extension of myself, of ends I had not yet imagined. In their high awareness they seemed to touch us all in our neglect. I was not alone on the beach. The earth had once again rescued me from exile.

Then a few people joined me who had walked in and were watching the birds. One of them, who had once shingled the roof of our house some twenty-five years before, had come with his family. He was the grandson of D. H. Sears, who ran an ice cream parlor we used to patronize; it had the best ice cream on the Cape. His wife was originally from Newfoundland and had lived on the shores of Witless Bay, overlooking a seabird colony. There was also a woman of Scottish and Dutch descent who had not forgotten her origins, where the sea winds blew along the coasts of Europe.

As they were admiring the birds, I felt as if the beach had now become a place for first landings again. We were all immigrants who had come to a revitalized part of a local shore that extended around the world.

Printed in the United States
By Bookmasters